7 00

The Chinese Way to a Long and Healthy Life

The Chinese Way
to
A Long and
Healthy Life

Prepared by Various Chinese Experts and
the Staff of the People's Medical Publishing House
of Beijing, China

BELL PUBLISHING COMPANY
New York

Publisher's Note

This book is *not* intended to be a do-it-yourself medical instruction manual. While a reader might find in these pages much valid information, to attempt self-diagnosis and/or treatment in the event of illness could be highly dangerous and could lead to further complications. In the event of illness the reader is strongly urged to see a doctor or other health care professional without delay.

This 1987 edition is published by Bell Publishing Company,
distributed by Crown Publishers, Inc.,
225 Park Avenue South, New York, New York 10003,
by arrangement with Hippocrene Books, Inc.

Printed and Bound in the United States of America

Library of Congress Cataloging-in-Publication Data

The Chinese way to a long and healthy life.

1. Exercise therapy—China.   2. Massage—China.
3. Health.   4. Medicine, Chinese.
I. Jen min wei sheng ch'u pan she.
RM725.C454   1987   613'.0951   87-1360

ISBN 0-517-64337-5

h g f

Contents

Publisher's Note

This volume, translated from the Chinese and amply illustrated, provides the precepts to longevity and healthy living that millions of Chinese live by in a daily routine of exercise, diet, and massage. The means to good health, passed down from generation to generation are presented in English for the Western reader.

In the section dealing with exercise, the reader is provided with simple instructions on how to maintain good health, how to prevent and treat pain afflicting various parts of the body, and how to prevent and ameliorate disease and prolong life.

Particularly striking is the new Qigong therapy containing specific exercises which the Chinese claim can prevent and cure cancer. Another valuable section, "The Simplified Taijiquan," according to the specialists who compiled this section, asserts that "regular practice of Taijiquan can not only strengthen health, promote vigorous vitality, but also prevent and cure, among other diseases, neurasthenia, ulcers, heart disease, and tuberculosis."

The diet section concludes with thirty recipes especially selected, after years of testing, because of their curative effect on many of the ills to which people are susceptible.

Introduction

China is a country with a long history and a rich cultural heritage. Over many generations, the Chinese people have created a number of effective techniques of physical exercise to improve health and increase the human life span. This volume presents in detail to the American reading public some of these traditional exercises and remedies which are still widely popular in China today. This book includes systems of physical training prepared by Master Gu Daifeng and Dr. Cao Xizhen, as well as the well-known "Eighteen Therapeutic Exercises," "Twenty Exercises for Treating Disease and Prolonging Life," Beijing *Qigong* Master Guo Lin's recent "New *Qigong* Therapy," and a simplified version of the traditional Chen family *Taijiquan*. Before each exercise there is a brief biographical sketch of the author and a simple theoretical introduction. The specific postures are illustrated by diagrams to make learning easier.

Each of these physical training techniques has different characteristics, and all of them are suitable for persons of any age or sex. The student may choose those exercises which suit his individual constitution and situation. In addition to the exercises, a total of thirty rare, traditional (and tasty!) Chinese medicinal and tonic recipes have been included for the reader's pleasure.

The Chinese Way to a Long and Healthy Life

I
Health-Care
Exercises

Various kinds of health-care exercises are quite popular in China and are widely practiced by the people. The exercises introduced in this chapter, written by two senior specialists in the field—Gu Daifeng and Cao Xizhen, include some of the most popular exercises of their kind.

Gu Daifeng is a native of Ji Nan, Shandong Province, China. As a young man, he studied day and night for the imperial examination, impairing his health in the process. By the time he reached middle age, the difficult life he had been compelled to lead, caused him to become even more run-down. Although not yet forty, his eyes were already failing and he frequently suffered from dizziness, pains in the back and legs and looked considerably older than his true age. Seeing this, his parents decided to teach him the health-care exercises that had been handed down in their family for generations. After less than half a year's practice, Gu's ailments were gone and he became quite strong. In the past thirty-odd years since then, he has never stopped doing the exercises, and at the age of seventy-eight he still has sharp ears and eyes. In order to pass on his knowledge to future generations and bring benefit to the people, he systematized, through his personal practice, these effective exercises which previously had been kept secret, handed down only in the family, and wrote a booklet entitled *Health-Care Massage*. The booklet became a bestseller in China and more than three million copies have been sold since its publication. The "Eight Exercises on Bed," "Six Exercises on the Floor" and "One-Hundred Pace Slow Walk" introduced in this book are reprinted from that booklet.

The "Eight Exercises on Bed" features massage which is done along certain Meridians* and acupuncture points. The "Six Exercises on the Floor" exercises primarily the upper limbs, but the functioning of the internal organs can be improved by its practice as well. "One-Hundred Pace Slow Walk" is basically an exercise of the lower limbs. Its movements are gentle and slow and the practitioner may repeat the exercise as much as he likes.

Cao Xizhen, once a specialist in the Massage Department of Beijing's Xuan Wu Hospital, mastered superb medical skills and was one of the best known senior doctors in traditional Chinese medicine in the city. By massaging along meridian points, he achieved good results in treating quite a number of complicated cases in both internal medicine and surgery. By persisting in doing the exercises all year round he kept fit and strong and had a ruddy complexion. At the age of seventy-eight, he was still busy working in the outpatient clinic and writing books, one of which, "Massage for Prevention and Treatment of Disease," has been highly praised by the reading public. The "Five Exercises on Bed" and the "Twelve Sitting Exercises on Bed" included in this book were written by Cao in accordance with the ancient art of massage and his personal experiences.

The "Five Exercises on Bed" is composed of exercises for several different prone positions and methods of self-massage. The "Twelve Sitting Exercises on Bed" are methods of exercise and massage that are best practiced before going to sleep at night and getting up in the morning.

The health-care exercises introduced here are simple, easy

---

*In Chinese medicine, meridians are regarded as passages through which vital energy circulates, and along which the acupuncture points are distributed.

to learn, do not take too much time, and can be practiced by anyone. As long as the practitioner is persistent, he can succeed in preventing many ailments and in prolonging his life.

Eight Exercises on Bed (*Chuangshang Baduanjin*)

Jin is the Chinese word for brocade woven of silk of various colors. The ancients compared the health-care exercises they created to beautiful and colorful brocades, and as these exercises consisted of eight sections (*Ba Duan*), they were called *Baduanjin*.

There are two types of *Baduanjin:* one to be done in a standing position and the other to be practiced sitting. The *Baduanjin* contained here is for the sitting position and focuses on massage.

While doing this series of exercises, the student must free his mind of distracting thoughts focusing his concentration on the navel. Breathing should be done by naturally expanding and contracting the abdomen, and must be slow, even, quiet, and fine. If performed properly, the student will feel comfortable, natural and relaxed.

1. DRY BATH

Functions:

This exercise improves blood circulation, unblocks the Meridians (called *Jingluo* in Chinese) and blood vessels, loosens the joints and aids in peristalsis. After doing this exercise, the student should feel physical well-being and be mentally refreshed. The effect is noticeable. To facilitate learning, this exercise has been divided into eight sections, A to H.

Fig. 1

A. HAND-RUB

Method:

1) Rub the palms together to warm them.
2) First grasp the back of the right hand tightly with the left hand and rub with force.
3) Grasp the back of the left hand tightly with the right hand and rub with force. Repeat at least ten times. (Rubbing once on the right hand followed by the left is taken as one time.) *(Fig. 1)*

According to traditional Chinese medical theory, the hands are the terminals of both the *Shousanyang* Meridian which extends from the head, and the *Shousanyin* Meridian, which starts from the chest. Therefore, it is from the hands that the dry bath begins.

Functions:

Hand-rubbing can harmonize the body's vital energy and blood circulation, make the fingers more sensitive and nimble, and help to clear the Meridians, thereby facilitating the following exercises.

B. ARM MASSAGE

Method:

1) Press the right palm tightly on the inner side of the left wrist.

2) Rub forcefully along the inner side of the arm up to the shoulder, past the shoulder and then along the outer side of the arm down to the back of left hand.

3) Repeat ten times. *(Figs. 2 and 3)*

4) Repeat the procedure for the right arm. (Running the hand up and down the arm is counted as one movement.)

Functions:

Arm massage loosens the joints and unblocks the Meridians so as to prevent arthritis and other pains from developing in the shoulders or arms. Rheumatism sufferers can benefit from this exercise as well. This massage may be repeated hundreds of times if necessary.

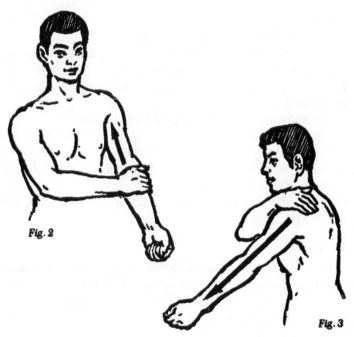

Fig. 2

Fig. 3

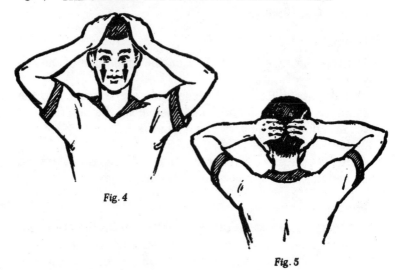

Fig. 4

Fig. 5

C. HEAD MASSAGE

Method:

1) Press both palms on the forehead.
2) Rub with a little force down to the chin, then up from the back of the head over the top of the head, returning to the forehead again. (The completion of this movement is taken as one time.)
3) Repeat over ten times. *(Figs. 4 and 5)*
4) Next rub the hair roots evenly and lightly with the fingertips or fingernails ten to twenty times. *(Fig. 6)*
5) Rub upward towards the top of the head with the thumbs from the temples *(Fig. 7)*.
6) At the top of the head, join the fingers and rub downward to the neck. *(Fig. 8)*

Functions:

Repeating the head massage over ten times will help lower blood pressure. For students whose blood pressure is excessively high, it is recommended to repeat the massage thirty to seventy times. (The completion of the above movements count as one time.)

Fig. 6

Fig. 7

Fig. 8

Note:

The head dominates the whole body. According to theories of traditional Chinese medicine, the head is where the body's *yang** gathers and where all blood vessels lead. Therefore, special attention needs to be paid to its protection. Massaging the head promotes the accumulation of *yang,* helps harmonize blood circulation and invigorates the body's energy and blood. A student who persists in practicing head massage will have a fine complexion even in old age.

In addition, as the hair follicles are connected with the capillaries, a light rubbing of the hair roots may improve circulation in the capillaries of the head, which can disperse congestion and improve the blood supply to the brain and cranial nerves. Frequently rubbing the hair roots might also partially cure baldness.

---

*In Chinese philosophy and medicine, the word *yang* is used to refer to the masculine or positive principle in nature. *Yin* refers to the female or negative principle.

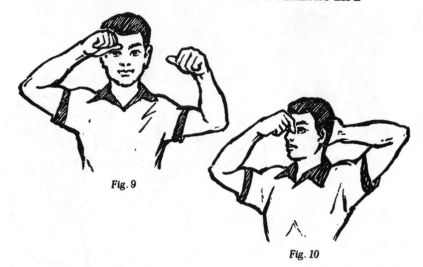

Fig. 9

Fig. 10

D. EYE MASSAGE

Method:

1) Clench both hands loosely with thumbs bent and rub the eyelids with the backs of the thumbs over ten times (*Fig. 9*).

2) Press the left thumb on the left temple, and the right thumb on the right temple, rub in a rotating movement ten times in both directions.

3) Pinch both sides of the nose where it joins the brow with the thumb and index finger of the right hand at least ten times. At the same time, rub with the left palm down the back of the head to the neck over ten times. (*Fig. 10*)

4) Change hands and repeat.

Function:

According to theories of the traditional Chinese medicine, the functioning of the eyes is related to the "five internal organs."* For this reason, the pupils of people suffering from renal diseases are usually dull-looking. This type of massage can facilitate the flow of vital energy and blood to the area

---

*heart, liver, spleen, lungs and kidneys

around the eyes, keep the muscles elastic and prevent the eyelids from sagging even in old age. In addition, eye massage can be of some help in preventing myopia and hypermetropia.

As there are numerous capillaries at the temples, massaging this area can clear and invigorate the Meridians there, resist chills, alleviate headaches and dizziness and generally promote a feeling of well-being.

Pinching the bridge of the nose where it joins the brow can rid the eyes of abnormal internal heat* and help prevent eye diseases.

E. NOSE MASSAGE

Method:

1) Bend the thumbs slightly and clench the other fingers loosely.

2) Rub forcefully with the back of the thumbs along both sides of the nasal bridge up and down ten times. *(Fig. 11)* (In winter or during a sudden change to cold weather, this massage may be repeated over thirty times.)

Fig. 11

*internal heat or fire is considered one of the six external factors which can cause disease according to Chinese medical theory. The other five are: wind, cold, summer heat, humidity and dryness. The particular form referred to here *(Xuhuo)* is characterized by symptoms such as insomnia, night sweats, dry throat, dizziness, ringing in the ears, etc.

Points to Remember:

When rubbing the nose, the thumbs can move up and down simultaneously, or with one thumb going up while the other goes down. (The movement from the nostrils up to the eyes and back down again is counted as one time.)

Function:

The rubbing of the sides of nose can invigorate circulation around the nasal cavity, maintain normal body temperature and reduce irritation of the lungs caused by cold air. Consequently, this exercise is helpful in getting rid of coughs and preventing colds.

F. CHEST MASSAGE

Method:

1) Place the right palm on the upper chest above the right breast, with fingers pointing downward.

2) Forcefully push the right palm down diagonally to the lower left.

3) Then push the left palm from above the left breast down diagonally to the lower right.

4) Alternate ten times each, left and right. (*Figs. 12 and 13*)

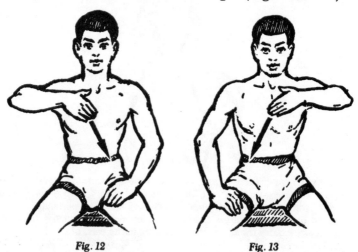

Fig. 12   Fig. 13

Function:

As the *Ren* Meridian, which commands circulation of the blood in the lungs, lies in the chest, and the chest contains both the heart and lungs, the rubbing of the chest can improve respiration, provide relief from asthma, prevent tracheitis, get rid of the ill effects of cold and internal heat* and keep the heart and lungs in good condition.

G. LEG MASSAGE

Method:

1) Hold the upper end of one thigh tightly with both hands and rub forcefully along the leg down to the anklebone and then back to the groin.

2) Repeat ten times (An up and down movement is counted as one time.)

3) Repeat for the other leg. *(Fig. 14)*

Fig. 14

*The symptoms of this particular type of internal heat (*Xinhuo*) include mental uneasiness, thirst and rapid pulse.

Note:

If it is difficult to rub the leg this way, rub the thigh and calf separately.

Function:

The important *Zusanyang* and the *Zusanyin* Meridians both pass through the leg. Therefore, leg massage can make the leg joints limber, strengthen the muscles and help prevent leg ailments.

H. KNEE MASSAGE

Method:

1) Press both palms on the knees tightly
2) Circle simultaneously ten times from the outside to the inside.
3) Repeat in the opposite direction. *(Fig. 15)*

Note:

If the student has knee trouble, he can put both palms on the affected knee and rub.

Fig. 15

Function:

Knees bear the bulk of the weight of body when in action. In addition, there are a lot of cartilage and ligament and fewer blood vessels at the knees. Therefore, they are most liable to diseases caused by damp cold and strain. Frequent knee rubbing can warm the knees, help them resist chill and invigorate the bones and muscles, thus strengthening the functioning of the knees and helping prevent such stubborn diseases as arthritis and rheumatism.

2. SOUNDING THE DRUM OF HEAVEN.

Method:

1) Press palms tightly over the ears and strike the occipital bone (by the cerebellum) lightly ten times with the index, middle and ring fingers of both hands.
2) Continue to press palms over the ears, keeping fingers tightly on the occipital bone.
3) Suddenly remove palms from ears.
4) Repeat ten times. *(Figs. 16 and 17)*
5) Put middle or index fingers into the ears, turn the fingers three times and remove suddenly.
6) Repeat three to five times. *(Figs. 18 and 19)*

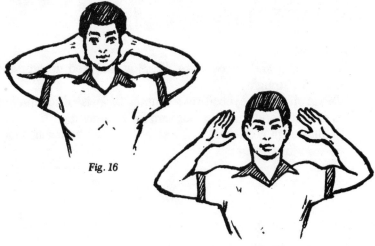

Fig. 16

Fig. 17

Fig. 18

Fig. 19

Function:

As all the Yang Meridians of the twelve Meridians meet inside the occipital bone, tapping it lightly can refresh the mind and improve memory. More tangible results can be achieved by practicing just after getting up in the morning or when feeling tired.

As the nerves of the ear vestibule are directly linked with the brain and the sudden covering and uncovering of the ears makes the ear drum vibrate, hearing power may be improved and ear diseases can be prevented by doing this exercise.

3. EYE ROTATION

Method:

1) Sit erect and concentrate, keeping the head upright and the waist straight.

2) Revolve both eyeballs in a counterclockwise direction five to six times and then look forward for a moment.

3) Repeat in a clockwise direction five to six times and look forward for a moment.

Function:

Rotating the eyeballs can build up the outer muscles of the eyes, increase the circulation of the fluids in the eyes and strengthen the functioning of the eye muscles, thus preventing eye strain, myopia and hypermetropia.

4. CLICKING THE TEETH

Method:

1) First keep the mind at ease and concentrate with the mouth lightly closed.
2) Then click the teeth together lightly thirty times.

Function:

The teeth are also closely linked with the functions of such internal organs as the stomach, intestines, spleen, kidney and liver. Therefore, the frequent clicking of the teeth strengthens the teeth and improves the functioning of the digestive system.

5. RINSING THE MOUTH

Method:

1) Close the mouth, keeping the teeth together.
2) Then move the cheeks and tongue in a rinsing motion.
3) Repeat thirty times.

Note:

When performing this exercise, much saliva is secreted. When the saliva fills the mouth, swallow it slowly in three gulps, one third each time. Beginners may not secrete much saliva, but persistence in practice will naturally result in increased salivation.

Function:

The purpose of this exercise is to increase salivation so as to aid digestion.

Fig. 20

6. RUBBING THE SMALL OF THE BACK

Method:

1) Rub palms first to warm them and place them tightly on both sides of the small of the back.

2) Rub forcefully down to the coccyx and then up to the highest place that can be reached. The completion of this movement is counted as one time.

3) Rub with force thirty times. (*Fig. 20*)

Function:

The small of the back is located on the Dai Meridian. (The Meridian which goes around the waist.) Located there are the kidneys, which need warmth and cannot tolerate chill. The rubbing of the lower back with palms is bound to give out warmth, thus the functioning of the kidneys are improved and the Dai Meridian is cleared. By persisting in doing this exercise the student's back will not become bent in old age and lumbago will be prevented as well.

7. ABDOMEN MASSAGE

Method:

1) Place the left hand on the waist or on the upper end of left thigh. (No special requirement for the placing of the hand if performed lying down.)

2) Rub with right palm from the lower left of the pit of stomach to the lower abdomen below the navel,

3) Turn right and up to the starting point. (This process is counted as one time.)

4) Repeat thirty times.

5) Repeat the process with hands reversed. (*Figs. 21 and 22*)

Note:

The rubbing of the abdomen must be light. As this exercise takes much time, those who have no gastro-intestinal troubles may leave it out or just repeat five to six times. Peristalsis follows a certain direction from top to bottom. However, as the intestines are coiled, their movement during the digestive process follows a spiraling pattern. Therefore, both the left and right abdomen may be rubbed thirty times each.

Fig. 21   *Fig. 22*

Function:

Long persistence in massaging the abdomen not only improves the digestive functions of the stomach and intestines but also helps with the treatment of gastro-intestinal diseases. This is because the rubbing of chest and abdomen applies pressure to the internal organs and the diaphragm muscles, causing them to move. As a result, the functioning of the stomach and intestines can be enhanced, the activities of various organs invigorated and metabolism can be increased, gradually eliminating the focus of infection if there is one, thus leading to recovery.

Note:

As women have different physiques, they should practice this exercise somewhat differently.

Method:

1) First rub the palms to warm them, then put the left hand on the waist or edge of thigh, with the thumb pointing forward, heel of hand supporting the lower back.
2) Rub with the right palm from the pit of stomach towards the lower left and circle back. One circle is counted as one time.
3) Repeat scores of times.
4) Reverse hands and rub with the left palm from the navel to the lower right, past the lower abdomen along the fringe of the pubic bone and back to the starting point. This is counted as one time.
5) Repeat scores of times.

Note:

The paths covered by the two palms are different: The right palm moves between the navel and the pit of stomach starting from the pit of stomach towards the lower left, while the left palm rubs and circles at the lower abdomen below the navel, starting from the navel going towards the lower right.

Function:

Persistence in doing this exercise can strengthen a woman's internal organs and viscera, help with digestion, regulate the menstrual cycle and build up vital energy.

8. RUBBING THE ARCHES OF THE FEET

Method:

1) Rub both hands to warm them.
2) Rub the arches of the feet eighty times each. *(Fig. 23)*

Function:

The foot arch belongs to the Lesser *Yin* Meridian of the leg, (the Kidney Meridian), which begins from the arch and stops at the top of the chest. This is the channel through which waste energy descends. Therefore, the rubbing of the arch of the foot can lead the abnormal heat *(Huhuo)* in the kidneys and the turbid energy in the upper body down and can improve the functioning of liver and eyes. Better results may be achieved if this exercise is done right after washing the feet.

Fig. 23

Six Exercises on the Floor

The movements of these exercises are derived from the *Yijinjing* (the *Classic of Muscle Change*) and the *Buduanjin* in standing position. If coordinated with the "Eight Exercises on Bed," results will be even greater. The "Eight Exercises on Bed" are mainly for massaging the whole body whereas the "Six Exercises on the Floor" can strengthen the limbs and the body and improve the functioning of the internal organs.

When doing this series of exercises, it is necessary to keep calm and concentrate the mind on the navel. Breathe naturally in concert with the movements, preferably through the nose. The breathing can also be done in such a way that the practitioner licks the roof of the mouth when inhaling and releases the tongue when exhaling, causing increased salivation which can increase vital energy. At the end of the exercises, the saliva must be swallowed.

1. ARM STRETCH

Method:

1) Stand upright and separate the feet to a distance equal to the width of the shoulders, with the toes slightly pointing inward.

2) Relax the upper body and bend the legs slightly, draw the buttocks inward, keeping the back straight.

3) Maintain the upper body in a state of light emptiness, shifting all weight to the lower body.

4) Look forward and focus the mind on the navel. (If it is too difficult to maintain this posture, keep the legs straight or stand freely.) *(Fig. 24)*

5) Raise both arms up to chest height slowly along the torso *(Fig. 25)*.

6) Reach out with both arms at shoulder level, with hands

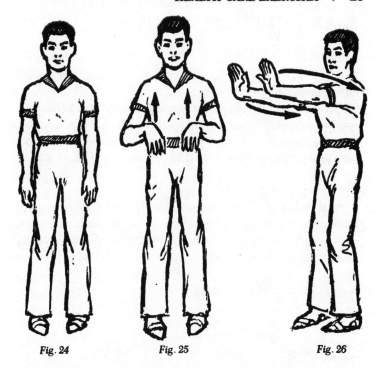

Fig. 24   Fig. 25   Fig. 26

bent upward at the wrist, fingers kept together and palms facing forward.

7) Stretch the muscles of both arms, wrists and fingers ten times. *(Fig. 26)*

Note:

When stretching, the arms should tremble slightly with the tensing and relaxing of the muscles, but the forward stretched posture and position of the arms do not change as the force is only inwardly exerted as in isometric exercise.

Function:

This exercise can clear the Meridians and improve the circulation of blood and vital energy in the hands and arms, which is also beneficial to the liver and eyes.

2. ARM SIDEWAYS STRETCH

Method:

1) Stretch out both arms sideways at shoulder level, palms facing upward.

2) Stretch the muscles of the shoulder, arms and hands sideways with invisible force for at least ten times. (When stretching, the shoulders shrug slightly, but the side-stretched posture and position of the arms do not change.) *(Figs. 27 and 28)*

Function:

As the neck is the passageway for the main artery and vein leading to the brain and for the cone of the central nervous system, this exercise, which moves the neck, has favorable effects on the brain. It also helps enlarge the capacity of the lungs.

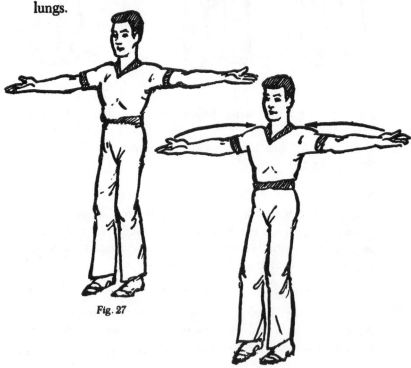

Fig. 27

Fig. 28

Fig. 29

Fig. 30

3. ARMS DOWN

Method:

1) Start from the previous position (in Exercise Two).
2) Move the hands back to the front of the chest and lower them naturally along the torso and the thighs, palms facing the floor, fingers pointing sideways.
3) While keeping this posture, push down ten times. (*Figs. 29 and 30*)

Note:

Remember to keep the arms straight and use only invisible isometric force.

4. ARM STROKE

Method:

1) Keeping waist and legs straight, lean the torso forward and face palms towards each other.
2) Move the arms across each other in a stroking motion with the hands.
3) Repeat ten times. *(Figs. 31 and 32)*

Note:

The stroking movement must be natural and smooth.

Function:

This exercise helps build up the lower back and kidneys.

Fig. 31

Fig. 32

5. ARMS UP

Method:

1) Start from the previous position in Exercise Four.
2) Bend both wrists so that palms are turned upward with fingertips nearly touching. *(Fig. 33)*
3) Raise hands up to the chest *(Fig. 34)*
4) Turn the palms upward as you raise the hands overhead, straightening the arms, keeping them a shoulder-width apart, fingers pointing at each other palms up.
5) Push up with invisible force ten times. *(Fig. 35)*

Function:

This exercise is beneficial to the *San Jiao* (Triple Warmer).*
According to traditional Chinese medical theory, the *San Jiao*

Fig. 33

Fig. 34

Fig. 35

*The three visceral cavities housing the internal organs in Chinese medicine.

is divided into three parts—the upper, middle and lower. The upper *Jiao* lies in the upper opening of the stomach,* the middle *Jiao* lies in the middle of the stomach and the lower *Jiao* in the upper opening of the bladder. There have always been different explanations concerning the position and function of the *San Jiao* and further study needs to be made.

6. HAND GRAB

Method:

1) With arms still overhead as in Fig. 35, reach forward with the left arm at shoulder level, making a fist and exert effort as if grabbing something *(Fig. 36)* and draw it back to the chest.
2) Reach out with the right hand at shoulder level, exert effort as if grabbing something *(Fig. 37)* and draw it back to the chest.
3) Finally do the same thing with both arms at shoulder level.
4) Repeat ten times with each arm.

Note:

Exert effort not only with the arms and wrists but with the whole body. The effort exerted makes the torso turn slightly left or right, causing the abdominal muscles to move forcefully. The knees may bend slightly while exerting effort. *(Fig. 38)*

Function:

This exercise can strengthen the arms and help improve the functioning of the spleen and stomach.

---

*Traditional Chinese medical terms such as "upper opening" of the stomach or bladder are unrelated in meaning to any concepts of Western anatomy, and are part of the Chinese theory of the three visceral cavities (upper, middle and lower).

Fig. 36

Fig. 37

Fig. 38

The One-Hundred Pace Slow Walk

This exercise, mainly for the lower limbs, can complement the "Six Exercises on the Floor" which exercise primarily the upper limbs.

The "One-Hundred Pace Walk" is extremely simple and very similar to normal walking. There are two ways of practicing it to meet the needs of different people; the first is slightly more difficult than the second.

Before beginning, dispel any distracting thoughts, refrain from listening to extraneous sounds or glancing sideways, and relax the whole body. Do the exercise gently and slowly and do not use force.

1. METHOD ONE

A. WALKING ARM RAISE

Method:

1) Stand erect with arms hanging down and feet a shoulder width apart. (*Fig. 39*)

2) Looking forward, touch the hard palate with the tongue. Breathe naturally through the nose, using abdomen as well as lungs.

3) Keeping fingers together, lift up both arms slowly, drawing an arc to the mouth and nose. At the same time slowly raise one knee to hip level with the calf hanging down and toes pointing downward. (*Fig. 40*)

4) Immediately lower the hands as if you were stroking a beard past the front of the chest and abdomen and return to the starting position. While lowering the hands, gently put down the up-raised leg. This is taken as one step. (*Fig. 40*)

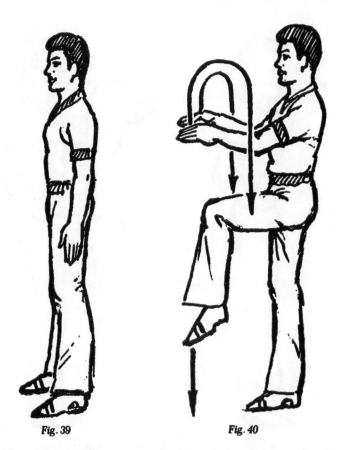

Fig. 39   Fig. 40

5) Repeat the same movement, raising and lowering the other leg. Take at least twenty steps. Then lower the tongue and swallow all accumulated saliva. Do not pause, or pause only briefly before going on to B.

B. RIGHT WALKING ARM RAISE

Method:

1) Touch the hard palate with the tongue. Put left hand on left hip with the thumb pointing backward, fingers pointing forward. (*Fig. 41*)

Fig. 41   *Fig. 42*

2) Slowly raise the right hand, drawing an arc up to the front of the mouth and nose, simultaneously raising one knee slowly to hip level. *(Fig. 42)*

3) Immediately, lower the right hand as if stroking a beard past the front of the chest and abdomen and return to the starting position. At the same time put the up-raised knee down slowly. This is taken as one step. *(Fig. 42)* Repeat with the other leg. Take twenty steps in this fashion. When finished, lower the tongue and swallow all accumulated saliva. Take a brief break or no break before going on to C.

C. LEFT WALKING ARM RAISE

Method:

Repeat B, raising the left hand.

D. ALTERNATE WALKING ARM RAISE

Method:

1) Raise and lower the left arm slowly as mentioned above, at the same time lifting and lowering the right leg for one step.

2) Repeat with right arm and left leg for another step.

3) Take approximately twenty steps in this fashion. When done, lower the tongue and swallow all accumulated saliva.

2. METHOD TWO

The movements are the same as in Method One, only the following key points are added:

1. Before and after raising one leg, the other leg should be kept slightly bent. (In Method One the other leg may remain straight.)

2. Relax and sink the shoulders, elbows and collarbone. This will cause the rib muscles to relax one by one. Draw the chest slightly inward (Do not overdo it) and stretch and lift up the back somewhat, but take care not to hunch up.

3. Relax the lower back and hips, drawing the coccyx inward as if propping up the lower abdomen. This helps the student keep a vertical line between head and torso.

Five Exercises on Bed

These exercises can be done any time of day or evening. The student may choose any one or all of the five positions and may increase or reduce the number of repetitions at will as long as no discomfort is felt.

1. SIDE LYING EXERCISE

Method:

1) Lie on side (doing exercise first on the right, then on the left).
2) If on the right side, bend the right arm, resting the right side of the face on the right hand.
3) Place the left arm along the left side of the body with the right leg straight and relaxed.
4) Bend the left leg, placing it over the right leg. *(Fig. 43)*
5) Breathe deeply three to five times.
6) Press on the left side at the waist with the left hand scores of times and massage obliquely downward along the abdomen and the lower abdomen scores of times. *(Fig. 44)*
7) Rub around the navel scores of times.
8) Massage and tap the left lower back with the heel of the left palm scores of times. *(Fig. 45)*

Function:

Stimulates the large and small intestines, bladder and kidneys; facilitates urination and excretion.

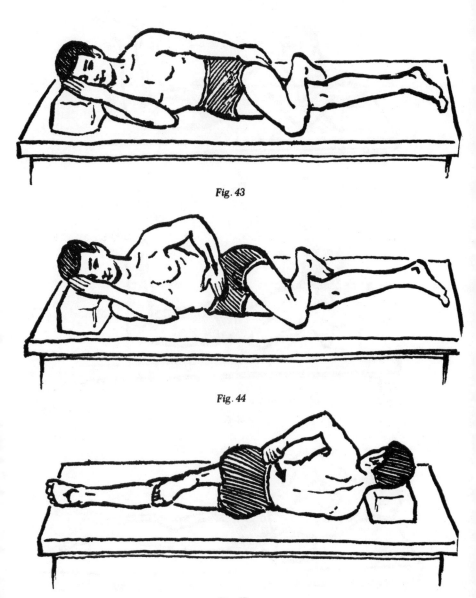

Fig. 43

Fig. 44

Fig. 45

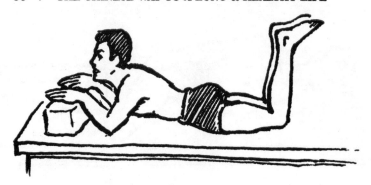

Fig. 46

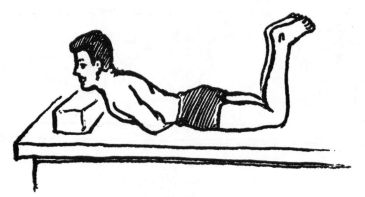

Fig. 47

Fig. 48

2. FRONT LYING EXERCISE

Method:

1) Lie face down with both hands on a pillow, the head slightly raised, legs bent at the knee. *(Fig. 46)*
2) Breathe deeply three to five times.
3) Put both hands successively under the upper abdomen, navel and the lower abdomen with palms up, taking three to five deep breaths in each position. *(Fig. 47)*
4) Place the pillow under the abdomen and push and rub the lower back with the hands ten times. *(Fig. 48)*

Functions:

Eases the *Ren* and *Du* Meridians; adjusts the functioning of the internal organs.

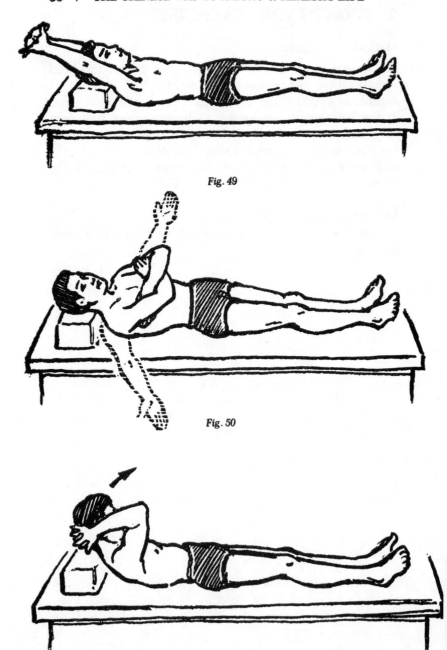

Fig. 49

Fig. 50

Fig. 51

3. BACK LYING EXERCISES

Method:

Lie on back, stretching the upper and lower limbs and breathe deeply three to five times. Then proceed with the following exercises:

1) Raise both arms from the sides up over the top of the head, clasp hands and turn the palms outward. Then breathe deeply three to five times and place the arms back along the sides. (Fig. 49)

2) Move both arms from the sides past the front of the face and stretch them sideways, breathe in deeply. Bend and cross arms in front of the chest. Then breathe out deeply. Repeat this exercise three to five times. (Fig. 50)

3) Clasp hands at the back of the head. Push the head forward attempting to make the chin touch the breastbone. Hold this position for a few seconds and return to the starting position. (Fig. 51) Repeat three to five times.

4) Abdomen Massage

a. Place the four fingers of each hand on the pit of the stomach and rub clockwise twenty to thirty times. (Fig. 52)

b. Place the four fingers of each hand on the pit of the stomach, rubbing clockwise, gradually moving the hands down below the navel. Repeat twenty to thirty times. (Fig. 53)

c. Place the left hand on the upper end of the left thigh and rub the stomach clockwise with the right hand twenty to thirty times. (Fig. 54)

d. Rub in a straight line with both hands from the pit of the stomach down to the pubic bone twenty to thirty times. (Fig. 55)

Functions:

Improves the functioning of the spleen, stomach, liver and gallbladder; helps digestion, regulates the functioning of the large and small intestines, reduces indigestion, eases bowel movements, increases oxygen supply to the organs and stops hiccups.

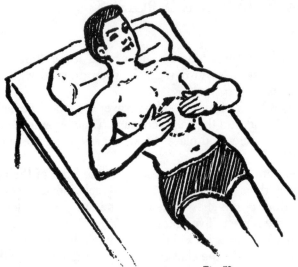

Fig. 52

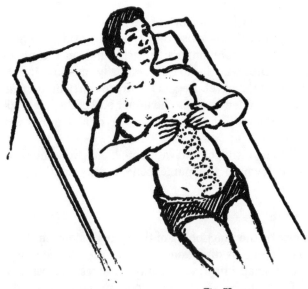

Fig. 53

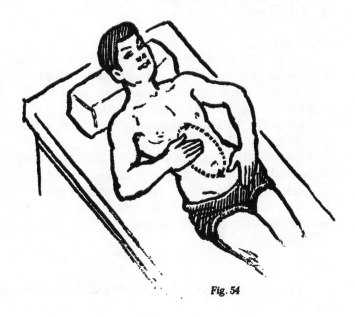

Fig. 54

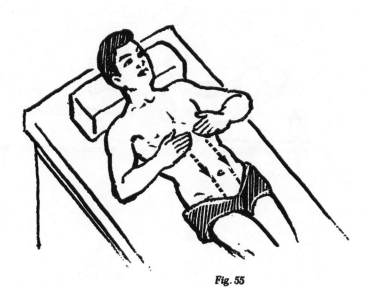

Fig. 55

4. LEG BEND

Method:

1) Lying on the back, breathe deeply, at the same time bending the left leg at knee and holding the left shin with both hands towards the chest. Do the same for the right leg and repeat three to five times. *(Fig. 56)*

2) Repeat No. 1 above, bending both legs simultaneously. *(Fig. 57)*

3) Raise both legs from the hips, then grasp the ankles with both hands and stretch the legs as fully as possible. *(Fig. 58)*

4) Raise both legs with knees bent. Grasping soles of the feet with both hands, lift up the torso and remain in this position for a few seconds. Repeat three to five times. *(Fig. 59)*

Functions:

Loosens the muscles and joints; improves circulation of the blood.

Fig. 56

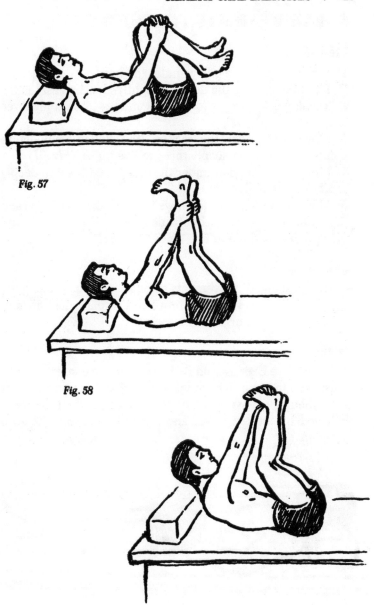

Fig. 57

Fig. 58

Fig. 59

5. EXERCISE WITH CUSHIONS

Method:

1) Lie on back with a pillow under the head.

2) Place the hands palm down, or tightly-clenched fists acting as "cushions", under the lower back and breathe deeply three to five times. (*Fig. 60*)

3) Move fists under the sacrum (the *Baliao* acupuncture points), and breathe deeply three to five times. (*Fig. 61*)

4) Move fists to a point under the coccyx and breathe deeply another three to five times.

5) Move the fists to a point between the thoracic vertebra and the lumbar vertebra, (the Bladder Meridian points), and breathe deeply three to five times. (*Fig. 62*)

Functions:

The "cushioned" movements stimulate the points along the Bladder Meridian so as to improve and regulate the functioning of the internal organs and viscera.

Note:

If the "Five Exercises on Bed" are to be done together, they must be done in a right to left order: first lying on the right side, then face down, then on the left side and on the back, followed by the leg bends and finally by the exercise with cushions.

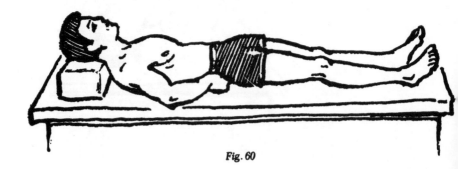

Fig. 60

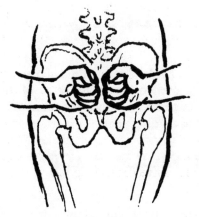

Fig. 61

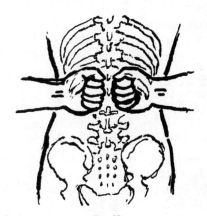

Fig. 62

Twelve Sitting Exercises on Bed

These exercises can be done at any time of day or evening. The student is free to choose any one or all of the twelve exercises and may increase or reduce the number of repetitions at will as long as no discomfort is experienced.

1. HEAD AND FACE MASSAGE

Method:

1) Rub the palms to warm them. Then rub the face with palms until the face feels warm. *(Fig. 63)*

2) Join the four fingers of each hand and massage the eyebrows (from the point of *Zanzhu* to the edge of hair passing the point of *Sikong*) and eye sockets scores of times. *(Fig. 64)*

3) Rub the outside of both nostrils with the index fingers or thumbs scores of times. *(Fig. 65)* Pinch the nasal septum and press the philtrum (the point of *Renzhong*) scores of times each. *(Fig. 66 (1) and (2))*

4) Close the mouth and click the teeth twenty to thirty times and swallow the accumulated saliva.

5) Spread and bend the fingers of each hand and do a combing movement from the forehead to the top and the back of the head scores of times. *(Fig. 67)*

6) Push down on the external ears from behind with the middle finger of each hand pushing the lobes forward. Spring the forefingers from over the middle fingers on to the mastoids. When doing this, a donging sound is heard. *(Fig. 68)* Repeat scores of times.

7) Push along and rub with one palm or both palms the front of throat, neck and the nape of the neck scores of times each. *(Fig. 69)*

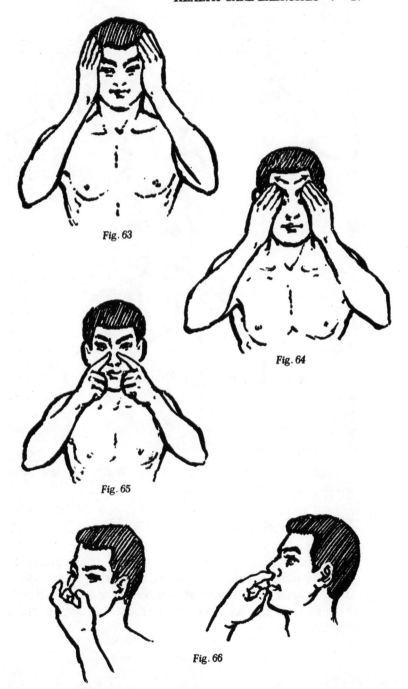

Fig. 63

Fig. 64

Fig. 65

Fig. 66

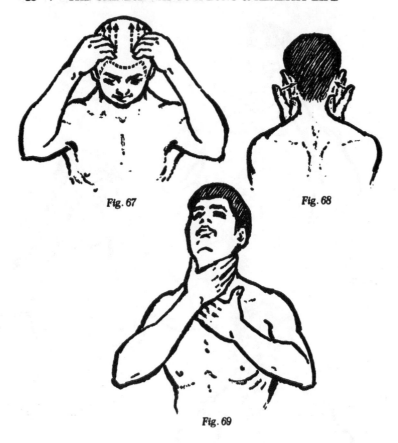

Fig. 67   Fig. 68

Fig. 69

Functions:

Improves vision, hearing, and functioning of the other sense organs; improves complexion.

2. LOOK BACK

Method:

1) Sit upright on bed, both palms flat on bed by your sides.
2) Turn head around as far as possible to the left and right in turn, and look up and down. Repeat scores of times each side. (*Fig. 70*)

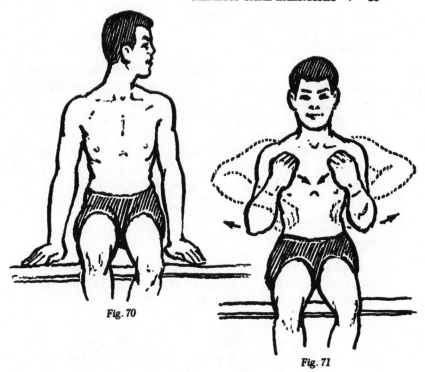

Fig. 70

Fig. 71

Note:

This exercise can also be done with arms raised naturally at shoulder level to both sides.

Functions:

Makes the neck flexible and improves the eyesight.

3. ELBOW AND ARM SWING

Method:

1) Bend the arms at the elbows and swivel back and forth, left and right. (Fig. 71)

Functions:

Strengthens the elbows and arms.

4. KNOCKING WRISTS

Method:

1) Keep fingers of both hands straight or clench them loosely. Knock the heel of one hand with the other, knocking the *Dailing* point and wrist bones. *(Fig. 72, no. 1)*

2) Knock the outside of both wrists together at the *Yangqi* point. *(Fig. 72, no. 2)*

3) Knock the first and second metacarpal bones of one hand with those of the other (the *Hegu* point). *(Fig. 72, no. 3)*

4) Knock the fifth metacarpal bone of one hand with that of the other (the point of *Hou Xi*). *(Fig. 72, no. 4)* Repeat twenty times each point.

Functions:

Prevents and cures swelling, numbness and weakness of the wrist, palm, hand and fingers; improves the functioning of the internal organs and viscera.

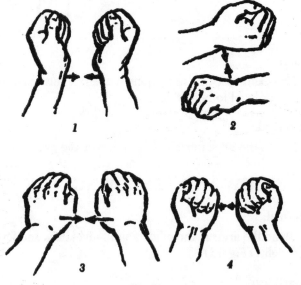

Fig. 72

5. FINGER EXERCISE

Method:

1) Spread the fingers of both hands and strike the part between thumb and index finger of one hand with that of the other.

2) Tap the spaces between the fingers of one hand with the fingertips of the other scores of times.

3) Reverse hands and repeat. (*Fig. 73*)

4) Knock the back and palm of one hand (the inner and outer *Laogong* points) with the other hand which is half clenched.

5) Reverse hands. Repeat scores of times for each hand. (*Fig. 74*)

Functions:

Makes fingers nimble; prevents and cures digital numbness and pain.

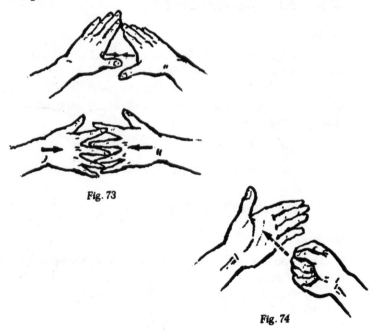

Fig. 73

Fig. 74

6. CATCHING AIR

Method:

1) Extend both arms forward in turn or together.

2) Move one hand or both hands as if you were catching something with force.

3) Draw back the catching hand to a point in front of the armpit on the same side (or to both sides if both arms move simultaneously), and take a deep breath. Repeat scores of times. (*Fig. 75*)

Functions:

Prevents and cures ailments of the shoulders and arms; adjusts the functioning of the heart, lungs, liver and gallbladder.

7. DRAWING THE BOW

Method:

1) Go through motions of drawing a bow on the left and right sides in turn.

2) At the same time turn the head and eyes in the direction of the shooting, accompanied with a deep breath. Repeat scores of times. (*Fig. 76*)

Functions:

Strengthens the shoulders and arms; stretches the chest.

8. RAISING ONE ARM

Method:

1) Raise one arm with palm facing up, taking a deep breath at the same time.

2) Repeat scores of times for each arm, inhaling on the way up, exhaling on the way down. (*Fig. 77*)

Fig. 75

Fig. 76

Fig. 77

Functions:

Strengthens the arms; adjusts the functioning of the spleen and stomach.

9. TAPPING THE SHOULDER AND WAIST

Method:

1) Tap the left shoulder with the right palm.
2) At the same time tap the right lower back with the back of the left hand.
3) Alternate and repeat scores of times on both sides. (*Fig. 78*)

Functions:

Prevents ailments of the shoulders and lower back.

10. SWINGING THE TORSO

Method:

1) Rest both hands naturally on the knees.

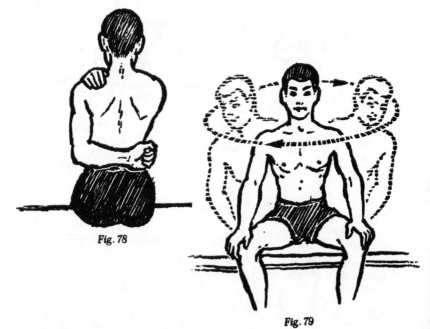

Fig. 78

Fig. 79

2) Circle the torso from left to right scores of times, breathing deeply. (*Fig. 79*)

Functions:

Limbers up the chest, abdomen and spine, regulates the vital energy and circulation of the blood.

11. KICKING

Method:

1) Sit with both legs stretched forward.
2) Bend one leg up towards the chest, clasping the knee with both hands.
3) Kick vigorously. Repeat scores of times with the left and right legs in turn. (*Fig. 80*)

Functions:

Strengthens the waist and legs; aids digestion.

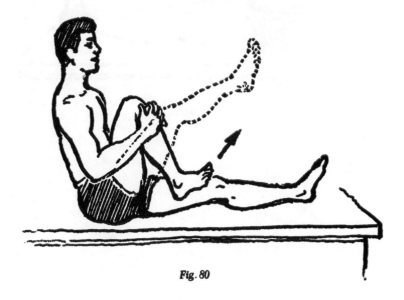

Fig. 80

12. PULLING TOES

Method:

1) In a sitting position, stretch forward both legs.
2) Lean the torso forward and try to pull the toes of both feet with the two hands. Repeat scores of times. *(Fig. 81)*

Functions:

Strengthens the lower back and kidneys.

Fig. 81

II
Eighteen Therapeutic Exercises

The "Eighteen Therapeutic Exercises" was compiled by the doctors of Dongchanglu Road Hospital, in the Huangpu District of Shanghai, in collaboration with the teachers of the Sports Medicine Research Group of Shanghai Sports Institute using as reference materials such Chinese traditional classics as: *Daoyin, Five-animal Exercises, Baduanjin,* and *Yijinjing.* Based on the pathology and pathogeny of neck, leg and shoulder pain and on traditional Chinese massage techniques, the "Eighteen Therapeutic Exercises" consists of six sets of exercises designed to prevent and treat pain in the neck, shoulders, buttocks, waist, legs, back, joints, tenosynovitis (inflammation of the tendon sheath), and functionary disorders of internal organs. Each set has its own special functions and peculiarities. The exercises are intended to improve blood circulation and nutrient supply in the muscle tissues of affected parts, speed up oxygenation and heal injured tissues. In other words, practicing these exercises can help either to cure diseases or prevent them, as the case may be.

Exercises to Prevent and Treat Pain in Neck and Shoulders

This set enables all joints of the neck, shoulders and fingers to function smoothly; improves circulation in soft tissues and enhances the regulatory function of the nerve secretions, relieves adhesion and spasm of muscle tissues and increases and revives muscle strength, enhancing its functioning. The exercises can also improve the functioning of the liver and cerebrum, and aid in digestion.

1. NECK STRETCH

Starting position:

Stand with feet apart slightly wider than shoulder width. Rest both hands at the waist with thumbs pointing backwards. *(Fig. 82)*

Movements:

1) Turn the head as far left as possible. *(Fig. 83)*
2) Return to starting position.
3) Turn head as far right as possible.
4) Return to starting position.
5) Bend the neck backward and look up.
6) Return to starting position.
7) Bend neck downward; look at ground.
8) Return to starting position.

Repeat the above movements two to four times each, to the count of eight each time.

Fig. 82

Fig. 83

Points to remember:

Keep the torso upright while bending neck and turning head. The chin should touch the chest while bending the neck downward.

Possible expected sensations:

Soreness and distension of neck muscles.

Functions:

Relieves acute neck sprains, tension and chronic ailments of the muscle tissues of the neck (Stiff neck).

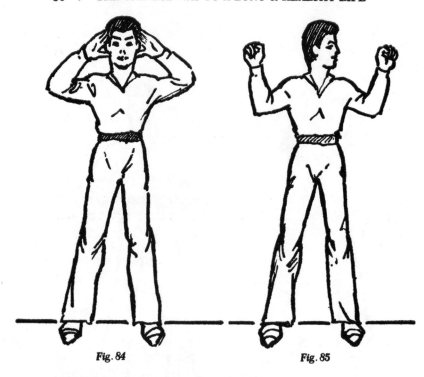

Fig. 84   Fig. 85

2. SHOULDER STRETCH

Starting position:

Stand with feet apart at a distance slightly wider than shoulder width. Raise hands over head with palms facing forward. (*Fig. 84*) Look straight ahead.

Movements:

1) Lower both arms to shoulder level and bend at the elbows. At the same time, clench fists loosely with knuckles facing backward. Turn the head to the left and look through hollow formed by the fist. (*Fig. 85*)
2) Return to starting position.
3–4) Repeat 1 and 2, reversing direction.
Repeat the above movements, two to four times to a count of eight each time.

Points to remember:

When separating the hands, keep the shoulders low and back, slightly protruding the chest. Maintain both elbows at the same level.

Possible expected sensations:

Relaxation in the chest. Soreness and distension in the muscles of the neck, shoulders and the back area.

Functions:

Relieves pain, stiffness and strain in the neck, shoulders, and back area. Relieves numbness in the arms and the stuffy feeling in the chest that accompanies colds, heartburn, and anxiety.

3. ARM STRETCH

Starting position:

Stand with feet apart at a distance slightly wider than shoulder width. Clench fists loosely and raise them up with elbows bent. The fists should be a bit higher than the shoulders, and so held that if the palms were exposed they would face forward. (*Fig. 86*)

Movements:

1) Open both fists and raise the arms with palms facing forward. Look at the fingers of the left hand. (*Fig. 87*)
2) Return to starting position.
3–4) Repeat 1 and 2, looking in the opposite direction.
Repeat two to four times, each time to a count of eight beats.

Points to remember:

While raising arms, thrust the chest forward and pull the abdomen in. Do not hold your breath.

Possible expected sensations:

Soreness and distension in the neck and waist.

Fig. 86

Fig. 87

Functions:

Relieves pain and tension in the neck, shoulders, back, waist; good for functional diseases in shoulder joints.

4. EXPANDING THE CHEST

Starting position:

Stand with feet apart at a distance slightly wider than shoulder width. Cross hands in front of the abdomen with the hand on the side of the affected shoulder on top. *(Fig. 88)*

Movements:

1) Raise the crossed hands with palms facing upward. Look at the back of hands.

2) Drop both arms to sides in a curving line, and return to starting position. Look straight ahead. *(Fig. 89)*

Repeat two to four times, each time to a count of eight beats.

Points to remember:

While raising arms, look up, thrust the chest forward and pull the abdomen in.

Possible expected sensations:

Soreness and distension in the neck, shoulders, waist, and lower back.

Functions:

Relieves pain in the neck, back and waist and stiffness in the shoulders.

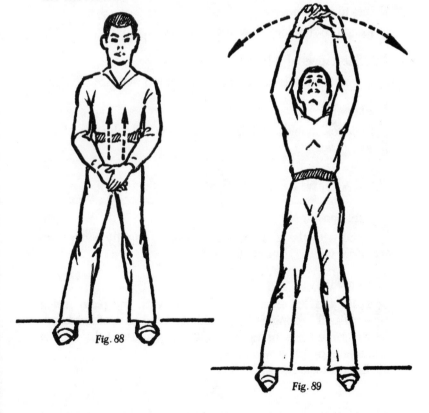

Fig. 88

Fig. 89

5. FLAPPING THE ARMS

Starting position:

Stand with the feet apart at a distance slightly wider than shoulder width. *(Fig. 90)*

Movements:

1) Bend the elbows and raise them a bit higher than the shoulders with the back of both hands facing each other, fingers pointing downward. Look to the left. *(Fig. 91)*
2) Lower elbows with palms facing each other in front of the face, slowly pressing downward. Return to starting position. *(Fig. 92)*
Repeat two to four times, each time to a count of eight beats.

Points to remember:

Keep the shoulders low and wrists relaxed.

Possible expected sensations:

Soreness and distension in the shoulders and ribs.

Functions:

Relieves shoulder stiffness and functional ailments of the arms.

6. RAISING ONE ARM

Starting position:

Stand with the feet apart at a distance slightly wider than shoulder width, arms at sides.

Movements:

1) Raise the left arm over the head with the palm facing upward as if propping the sky. Look at the back of left hand. At the same time, bend the right elbow and rest the back of right palm on the lower back. *(Fig. 93)*
2) Return to starting position.

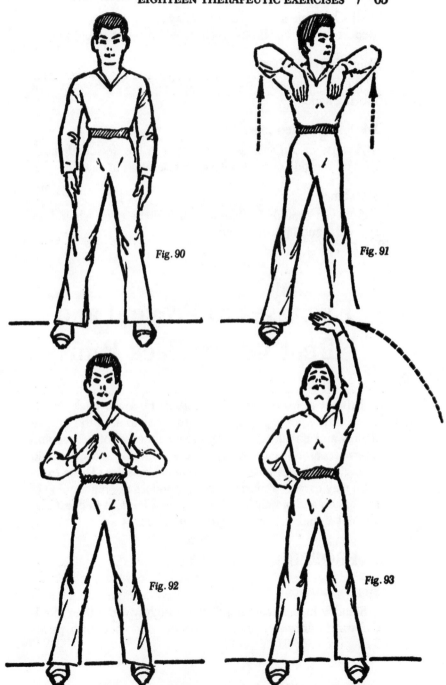

Fig. 90

Fig. 91

Fig. 92

Fig. 93

3–4) The same as 1 and 2, reversing arms.
Repeat two to four times, each time to a count of eight beats.

Points to remember:

When raising arm, keep it straight and keep the eyes on the moving hand.

Possible expected sensations:

A sense of soreness and distension in the neck and shoulders on the side of the raised arm; relaxation in chest.

Functions:

Relieves shoulder stiffness, pains in the neck, shoulders, and waist and improves digestion.

Exercises to Prevent and Treat Lower Back Pain

This set of exercises makes limber the lower back, waist, spine and os coxae joints; improves circulation in the muscle tissues and enhances the regulatory function of nerves and internal secretions; relieves muscular adhesion and spasm and strengthens lower back and abdomenal muscles. These exercises may correct abnormal spine, regulate the functioning of the spleen and stomach, relieve bloated feelings in chest and abdomen, and strengthen kidney function.

1. PROPPING THE SKY

Starting position:

Stand with feet apart at a distance slightly wider than shoulder width. Interlock fingers at upper abdomen with palms facing up. (*Fig. 94*)

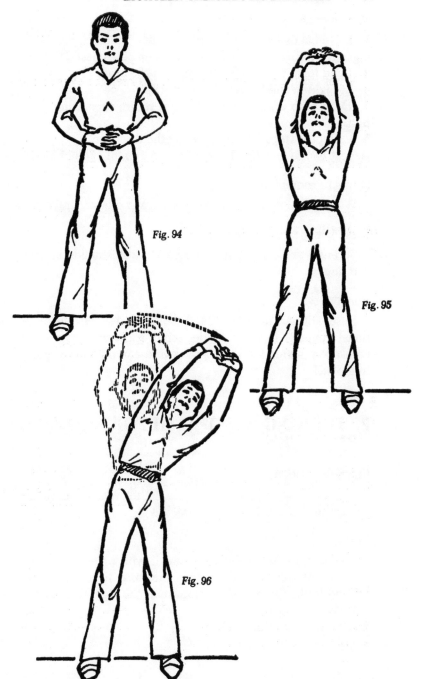

Fig. 94

Fig. 95

Fig. 96

Movements:

1. Raise hands over head, turn the palms up and push, looking at the back of the hands and expanding the chest. *(Fig. 95)*
2. Bend torso to the left, leading with the arms. *(Fig. 96)*
3. Straighten and bend to the left again.
4. Drop both arms to the sides and return to starting position.
5–8. Repeat steps 1 to 4, reversing the direction.
Repeat two to four times, each time to a count of eight beats.

Points to remember:

When pushing hands up, keep torso and elbows straight.

Possible expected sensations:

Soreness and distension in the neck, waist, shoulders, arms and fingers.

Functions:

Eases stiffness of the neck and shoulders, relieves the functional ailments in the shoulder joints and spine, corrects a crooked spine (or *kyphosis,* a backward curving of the spine, humpback).

2. TURNING WAIST WITH FORWARD ARM EXTENSION

Starting position:

Stand with feet apart at a distance slightly wider than shoulder width. Rest fists at waist. *(Fig. 97)*

Movements:

1. Open right fist and push forward, with palm also facing forward. At the same time, turn the torso to the left, also looking back. Keep the left elbow and the right arm on the same level. *(Fig. 98)*
2. Return to starting position.

Fig. 97

Fig. 98

3–4. The same as in 1 and 2 reversing arms and direction. Repeat two to four times, each time to a count of eight beats.

Points to remember:

While turning torso, keep legs straight and feet on the floor.

Possible expected sensations:

Soreness and distension in the waist, shoulders, neck and back.

Functions:

Helps heal injuries of muscle tissues in the neck, shoulders, back and waist; relieves numbness and muscular atrophy in the arms caused by neck and lower back pain.

Fig. 99

Fig. 100

3. ROTATING THE WAIST

Starting position:

Stand with feet apart at a distance slightly wider than shoulder width. Rest both hands at the waist with thumbs forward. *(Fig. 99)*

Movement:

1–4. Push forcefully with both hands the pelvis, causing it to rotate in a clockwise direction. *(Fig. 100)*

5–8. The same as in 1 to 4 rotating the pelvis in a counterclockwise direction.

Repeat two to four times, eight beats clockwise, eight beats counter-clockwise.

Points to remember:

Gradually increase the circumference of the rotations, keeping the legs straight, feet flat on the floor. When rotating forward, support waist with the hands.

Possible expected sensations:

Soreness and distension in waist and lower back.

Functions:

Relieves chronic lower back pain and acute pain caused by sprains in lower back. Relieves pain in lower back caused by occupations which require constant maintenance of body positions deleterious to the back.

4. FORWARD BEND

Starting position:

Stand with feet apart at a distance slightly wider than shoulder width. Cross the hands in front of abdomen with the affected hand on top, palms facing body. *(Fig. 88)*

Movements:

1) Raise both hands upward with palms facing forward. Look at the back of the hands. Expand chest and pull abdomen in. *(Fig. 101)*
2) Drop arms to shoulder level, palms facing up. *(Fig. 102)*
3) Turn the palms down, bend forward and downward with fingers touching the ground. *(Fig. 103)*
4) Cross the forearms in front of the body. *(Fig. 104)*
5–8) Repeat 1 to 4, returning to the starting position on the final beat.
Repeat two to four times, each time to a count of eight beats.

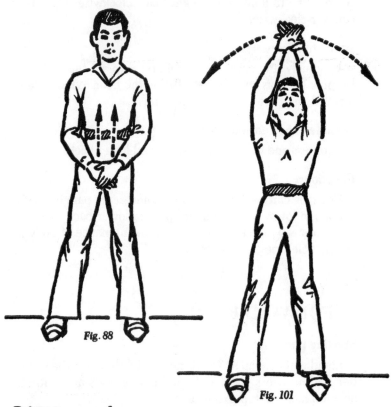

Fig. 88

Fig. 101

Points to remember:

Keep the legs straight and try to touch the ground with the fingers.

Possible expected sensations:

Soreness and distension in the waist, lower back and back of the legs.

Functions:

Relieves pain in the neck, back and waist.

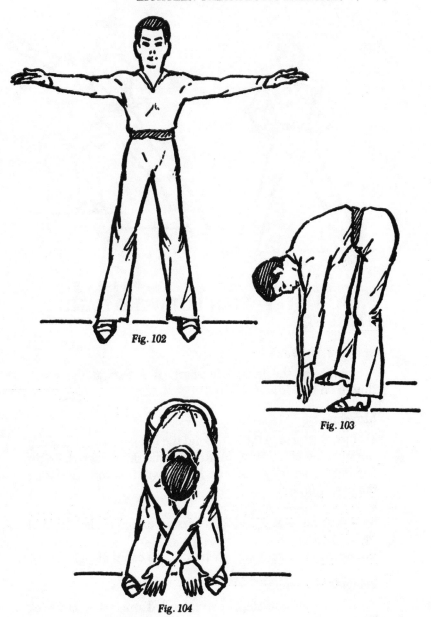

Fig. 102

Fig. 103

Fig. 104

Fig. 106

Fig. 105

5. BOW STEP WITH FORWARD HAND THRUST

Starting position:

Stand with the feet wide apart. Rest fists at the waist, thumb on top. *(Fig. 105)*

Movements:

1) Turn the torso to the left. Bend the left knee and straighten the right leg (left bow step). At the same time, open the right fist and thrust it forward, slightly upward, with palm facing the left. *(Fig. 106)*
2) Return to starting position.
3–4) The same as 1 and 2, reversing direction, left leg and right arm forward.

Repeat two to four times, each time to a count of eight beats.

Points to remember:

In taking the bow step, keep extended arm, spine, and back leg straight.

Fig. 108

Fig. 107

Fig. 109

Possible expected sensations:

Soreness and distension in lower back, waist and legs.

Functions:

Relieves pain and numbness in the neck, lower back, waist, arms, and legs.

6. STRETCH AND TOUCH FEET

Starting position:

Stand straight, feet together, arms at sides. *(Fig. 107)*

Movements:

1) Interlock the fingers in front of the upper abdomen with palms facing upward. Turn and stretch the hands upward past the face with palms facing up. Look at the backs of the hands. *(Figs. 108 and 109)*

Fig. 110

2) Bend forward and downward until the palms touch the feet. (*Fig. 110*)

3) Return to starting position.

Repeat two to four times, each time to a count of eight beats.

Points to remember:

When bending forward, move the buttocks slightly backward and keep the legs straight. Try to touch the feet with the palms.

Possible expected sensations:

Soreness and distension in the neck, lower back, waist, and legs.

Functions:

Helps cure injuries of the muscle tissues of the lower back, waist and legs, relieves stiffness of the lower back and waist; corrects side-bent spine (Kyphoscoliosis); relieves pain and numbness in the legs.

Exercises to Prevent and Treat Pains in Hips and Legs

These exercises can strengthen the muscles of the lower back, waist, abdomen, hips, buttocks and legs; relieve adhesion and spasm of the muscles of the hips, buttocks and legs, and correct abnormal formations of spine and pelvis.

1. ROTATING THE KNEES

Starting position:

Stand straight, feet together, arms at sides; bend forward, placing hands on knees, with eyes looking slightly forward. (*Fig. 111*)

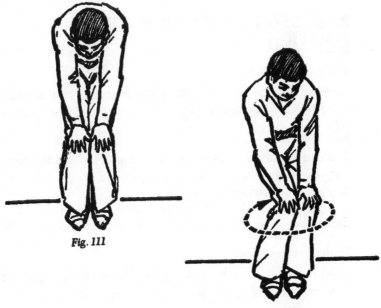

Fig. 111

Fig. 112

Movements:

1–4. Bend both legs at the knee and rotate once clockwise, straightening the legs when a half-circle has been completed, bending again to complete the rotation. *(Fig. 112)*

5–8. The same as 1 to 4 counter-clockwise.

Repeat two to four times, each time to a count of eight beats clockwise and eight beats counter-clockwise.

Points to remember:

Rotate the knees as much as possible.

Possible expected sensations:

Soreness and distension in the knees and ankles.

Functions:

Relieves pains and prevents weakness in the knees and ankles.

2. TORSO TURN IN SIDE LUNGE POSITION

Starting position:

Stand with the feet wide apart, hands resting on the waist, thumbs facing back. *(Fig. 113)*

Movements:

1. Bend the left leg shifting all weight onto it. Turn the torso forty-five degrees to the right. *(Fig. 114)*

2. Return to starting position.

3–4. The same as 1 and 2, but reversing the direction.

Repeat two to four times, each time to a count of eight beats.

Points to remember:

When bending the knee, keep it on line with the tips of the toes. Keep the torso upright.

Fig. 113

Fig. 114

Possible expected sensations:

Soreness and distension in the legs and thighs.

Functions:

Relieves pain in the lower back, waist, hips, and legs; eases stiffness in knees and ankles.

3. BOW, SQUAT, AND STRETCH

Starting position:

Stand straight, feet together, arms at sides.

Movements:

1. Bend forward with both hands resting on the knees, legs straight. (*Fig. 115*)

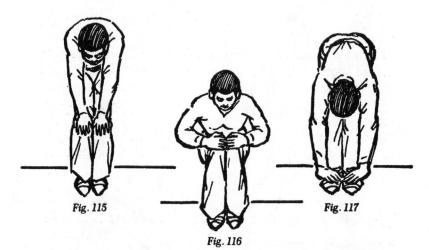

Fig. 115

Fig. 116

Fig. 117

2. Bend the knees and squat down, hands still resting on the knees, fingers now pointing to each other. *(Fig. 116)*
3. Place palms on insteps and straighten the legs. *(Fig. 117)*
4. Return to starting position.
Repeat two to four times, each time to a count of eight beats.

Points to remember:

Try to touch the insteps with the palms.

Possible expected sensations:

Soreness and distension in the knees, legs and thighs.

Functions:

Relieves stiffness in the lower back, waist, and knees; strengthens the leg muscles; eases discomfort in the legs due to muscular atrophy.

4. PROPPING THE SKY WITH ONE HAND ON KNEE

Starting position:

Stand with feet a shoulder-width apart.

Movements:

1. Bend the torso forward with the right hand resting on the left knee. (*Fig. 118*)

2. Straighten torso a bit. Raise the left hand across the front of the body and lift up over the head, the palm facing up and fingers pointing to the right. Look at the back of the left hand. Bend the knees slightly keeping the weight centered between the legs. (*Fig. 119*)

3. Bend torso forward again bringing left hand down, straightening legs and place the left hand on the right knee. (*Fig. 120*)

4. Return to starting position.

5–8. The same as 1–4, reversing arms.

Repeat two to four times, each time to a count of eight beats.

Points to remember:

While bending the knees, keep the feet flat on the ground and the torso upright.

Fig. 118

Fig. 120

Fig. 119

Possible expected sensations:

Soreness and distension in the neck, shoulders, lower back, waist and legs.

Functions:

Relieves pains and stiffness in the neck, shoulders, waist, lower back and legs.

5. HOLDING KNEE TO CHEST

Starting position:

Stand straight, feet together, arms at sides.

Movements:

1. Move the left foot one step forward, shifting all weight onto it. Lift the right heel off the ground and at the same time, push the hands straight upward with palms facing each other. Look up and expand chest. (*Fig. 121*)

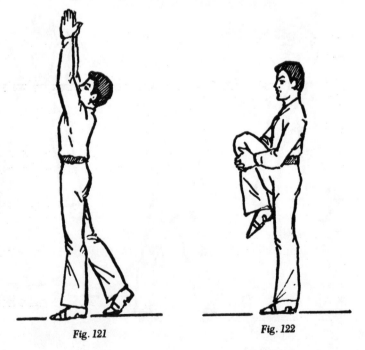

Fig. 121   Fig. 122

2. Drop the hands to the sides and at the same time, bend the right leg forward and up. Hold it at the knee with both hands and draw it to the chest. Keep the left leg straight. *(Fig. 122)*

3. Return to position 1.

4. Return to starting position.

5–8. The same as 1–4, reversing legs.

Repeat two to four times, each time to a count of eight beats.

Points to remember:

Stand firmly; draw the knee as close as possible to the chest and keep the standing leg straight.

Possible expected sensations:

Soreness and distension in the leg muscles.

Functions:

Relieves pain and stiffness in the buttocks and legs.

6. STROLLING

Starting position:

Stand straight, feet together with hands resting on waist, thumbs pointing back. *(Fig. 123)*

Movements:

1. The left foot takes one step forward with the heel landing first. Lift the right heel off the ground and shift all weight onto the left leg. *(Fig. 124)*

2. Lower the right heel, slightly bending the right knee. Shift weight onto the right leg and lift the sole of the left foot, with the heel remaining on the ground. *(Fig. 125)*

3. Take one step forward with the right foot and shift weight onto the right leg. Lift the left heel off ground.

4. Lower the left heel, slightly bending the left knee with weight shifted onto the left leg. Lift the sole of the right foot (with heel remaining on the ground).

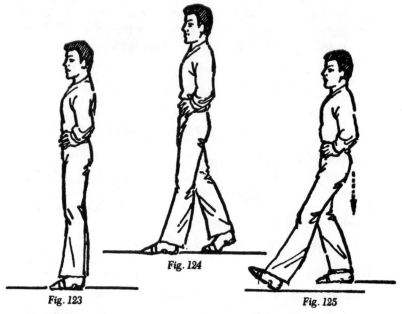

Fig. 123

Fig. 124

Fig. 125

5. Shift weight onto the right leg and lift the left heel off the ground.

6. Shift weight onto the left leg with left knee slightly bent. Lift the right sole, heel still on the ground.

7. Straighten the left leg and move the right foot one step backward with the right knee slightly bent. Shift weight onto the right leg.

8. Return to the starting position.

Repeat two to four times, each time to a count of eight beats.

Points to remember:

Keep the torso upright. While stepping forward, look ahead with the chest out.

Possible expected sensations:

Soreness and distention in legs and ankles.

Functions:

Relieves pain and stiffness in the legs, knees and ankles.

Exercises to Prevent and Treat Pains in Joints

These exercises improve cardiovascular functioning and enhance the regulatory function of the nerves; increase muscle power of the legs and arms, and keep the limbs in good condition. Performing these exercises also relieves adhesion and spasm of muscle tissues in the legs and arms. This set affects the entire body.

1. PUSHING PALMS IN RIDING STANCE

Starting position:

Stand upright with fists resting at the waist.

Movements:

1. Part feet to a distance slightly wider than shoulder width and bend the knees as if riding a horse. Push arms outward and turn the forearms inward. Push open palms forward, fingers pointing at each other. *(Fig. 126)*

2. Return to starting position.

Repeat two to four times, each time to a count of eight beats.

Points to remember:

When pushing palms forward, bend the wrists as far as possible and keep the arms straight.

Possible expected sensations:

Soreness and distension in the wrists and thighs.

Functions:

Relieves pain in the legs, arms, and knees.

Fig. 126   *Fig. 127*

2. CROSSED LEGGED KNEEBEND WITH PALM PUSHED SIDEWAYS

Starting position:

Stand with feet slightly apart with fists resting at the waist.

Movements:

1. Turn the body to the right, cross the right leg over the left leg and squat bringing left knee to kneeling position. At the same time, push the left arm to the left, palm out and look towards the right shoulder. *(Fig. 127)*
2. Return to starting position.
3–4. The same as 1 and 2, but reversing legs and direction. Repeat two to four times, each time to a count of eight beats.

Points to remember:

Keep the torso upright and steady.

Possible expected sensations:

Soreness and distension in the knees, legs and arms.

Functions:

Relieves pain in the arm and leg joints, neck, waist, and back.

3. UPWARD ALTERNATE ARM PUSH

Starting position:

Stand straight with half-clenched fists at the waist with palms facing upward. *(Fig. 128)*

Movements:

1. Open the right fist and lift it upward with the palm facing up. Look at the back of right hand. *(Fig. 129)*

Fig. 128

Fig. 129

Fig. 131

Fig. 130

2. Turn the torso ninety degrees to the left. *(Fig. 130)*
3. Drop the right palm and bend forward, touching the outside of the left foot with the right palm. *(Fig. 131)*
4. Turn to the right and move the right palm to the right instep. Return to starting position, raising the right palm upward along the outside of the right leg.
5–8. The same as 1–4, using the left arm in the opposite direction.
Repeat two to four times, each time to a count of eight beats.

Possible expected sensations:

Soreness and distension in the shoulders, arms, lower back, waist, and legs.

Functions:

Relieves pain in the shoulders, waist, back and legs.

4. TURN AND LOOK BACKWARD

Starting position:

Stand with the feet wide apart, fists at waist.

Movements:

1. Move the left foot one step forward. Bend the left knee and keep the right leg straight. Turn the torso to the left and look at the left shoulder. At the same time, push the right palm forward and slightly upward. Keep the right palm and the right leg on a straight line. *(Fig. 132)*
2. Return to starting position.
3–4. The same as 1–2, reversing arms and legs.
Repeat two to four times, each time to a count of eight beats.

Points to remember:

Keep the heel of the rear leg on the ground.

Fig. 132

Possible expected sensations:

Soreness and distension in the neck, shoulders, lower back, waist, and legs.

Functions:

Relieves pain and soreness in the arm and leg joints, neck, waist, and back.

5. DOWNWARD KICK

Starting position:

Stand with the feet a shoulder-width apart with hands resting at the waist, thumbs pointing backward.

Fig. 133

Fig. 134

Movements:

1. Lift the left leg with the knee bent, toes pointing upward and kick down with force towards the front of the right foot. *(Figs. 133–134)*
2. Return to starting position.
3–4. The same as 1–2, with the right foot.
Repeat two to four times, each time to a count of eight beats.

Points to remember:

Kick down firmly with energy going through the heel.

Possible expected sensations:

Soreness and distension in the legs.

Functions:

Relieves pain in the legs and knees.

6. KICKING THE SHUTTLECOCK

Starting position:

Stand straight with hands resting at the waist, thumbs pointing back.

Movements:

1. Lift the left leg with the knee bent and kick up and to the right. Return to starting position. *(Fig. 135)*
2. Lift the right leg with the knee bent and kick up and to the left. Return to starting position. *(Fig. 136)*
3. Lift the left leg with the knee bent and kick out to the side. Return to starting position. *(Fig. 137)*
4. Lift the right leg with the knee bent and kick out to the side. Return to starting position. *(Fig. 138)*
5. Lift the left leg with the knee bent and kick forward. Return to starting position. *(Fig. 139)*

Fig. 135

Fig. 136

Fig. 137

Fig. 138

Fig. 139

Fig. 140

6. Lift the right leg with the knee bent and kick forward. Return to starting position. *(Fig. 140)*

7. Bend the left knee and kick backward with the heel toward the buttocks. Return to starting position. *(Fig. 141)*

8. Bend the right knee and kick backward with the heel toward the buttocks. Return to starting position. *(Fig. 142)*

Repeat two to four times, each time to a count of eight beats.

Points to remember:

When kicking backward with the heel, keep the standing leg straight.

Possible expected sensations:

Soreness and distension in the legs.

Functions:

Relieves pain and distension in the hips and knees; strengthens the legs.

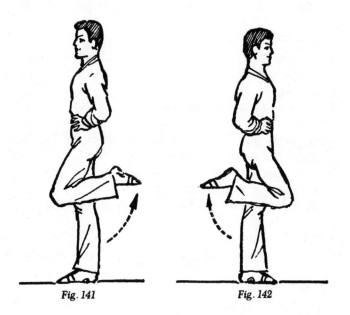

Fig. 141   Fig. 142

Exercises to Prevent and Treat Tenosynovitis

These exercises limber the joints, improve blood circulation and the regulatory function of the nerves, muscle tissues of the upper limbs, relieve adhesion and spasm of muscle tissues in the shoulders, arms, and fingers. They also prevent and relieve, to a certain extent, tennis elbow and tenosynovitis of the wrist and fingers.

1. PUSHING HANDS

Starting position:

Stand with feet apart at a distance slightly wider than shoulder width with hands at the front of waist, palms up.

Movements:

1. Push hands upward with palms up, fingers pointing toward each other, thumbs forward. Look at the back of the hands. *(Fig. 143)*
2. Return to starting position.
3. Turn torso to the left and push both hands to the sides with palms facing out. Look at the back of left hand. *(Fig. 144)*
4. Return to starting position.
5. The same as those in 3 to the right.
6. Return to starting position.
7. Push both hands to the sides with palms facing out. *(Fig. 145)*
8. Return to starting position.
Repeat two to four times, each time to a count of eight beats.

Points to remember:

Keep torso upright and feet flat on the ground.

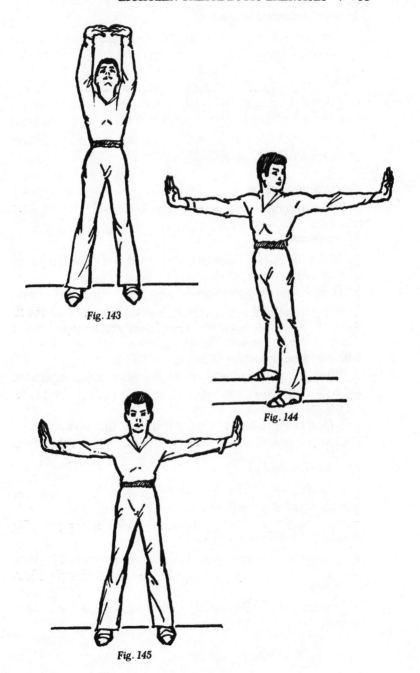

Fig. 143

Fig. 144

Fig. 145

Possible expected sensations:

Soreness and distension in the neck, shoulders, elbows, wrists and fingers.

Functions:

Relieves pain in the neck, shoulders, lower back and waist; eases tennis elbow and tenosynovitis of the wrist and fingers.

2. DRAWING A BOW

Starting position:

Stand straight, feet together, arms at sides.

Movements:

1. Move the left foot one step to the left and cross the palms in front of the chest, elbows slightly bent. *(Fig. 146)*
2. Bend knees to form a horse-riding position and at the same time, push the left arm to the left, palm facing left. Look at the back of the left hand, while raising the right arm in front of chest, pulling it back, as if drawing a bow with the right hand half-clenched, knuckles facing upward. *(Fig. 147)*
3. Press the palms downward at the same time, straighten the legs. *(Fig. 148)*
4. Return to starting position.
5–8. The same as 1–4, reversing arms and direction.
Repeat two to four times, each time to a count of eight beats.

Points to remember:

In performing 2 and 3, protrude the chest to press the shoulder blades towards the spine.

Possible expected sensations:

Soreness and distension in the forearms, wrists and fingers.

Functions:

Relieves tennis elbow and tenosynovitis of the wrists and fingers.

Fig. 146

Fig. 147

Fig. 148

3. STRETCHING WRIST TWIST

Starting position:

Stand with the feet apart at a distance slightly wider than shoulder width, fists at the waist, knuckles down.

Movements:

1. Open the fists and push upward with the palms facing each other. Look upward. *(Fig. 149)*

2. Clench fists, drop the arms to the sides, returning to the starting position.

Repeat two times, each time to a count of eight beats.

3. Open fists and straighten arm downward with palm facing forward. Raise hands above head with palms facing each other and look upward. *(Fig. 150)*

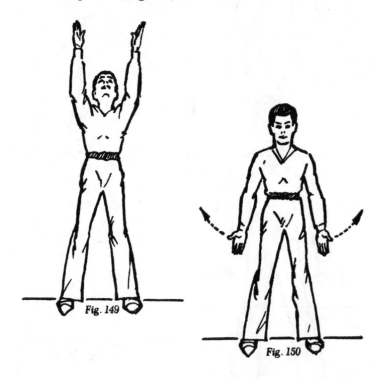

Fig. 149

Fig. 150

4. Bend the elbows and drop fists to sides past chest to return to starting position. *(Figs. 151–152)*

Repeat one to two times to an eight-beat count.

Repeat all 4 steps together, two to four times to an eight-beat count.

Points to remember:

When raising hands, expand the chest.

Possible expected sensations:

Soreness and distension in the wrists, elbows, shoulders and arms.

Functions:

Relieves stiffness of the shoulders, tennis elbow and tenosynovitis of the wrists and fingers.

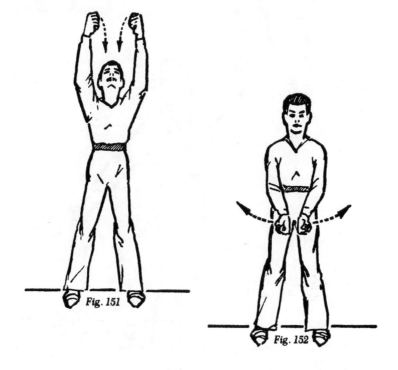

Fig. 151

Fig. 152

4. DIAGONAL ARM STRETCH

Starting position:

Stand with the feet apart at a distance slightly wider than shoulder width with fists at waist.

Movements:

1. Open the right fist and push it obliquely upward with the palm facing forward and the thumb pointing out. At the same time, extend the left arm backward, turning the forearm so that the knuckles face downward. Look at the left fist. (*Fig. 153*)
2. Return to starting position.
3–4. The same as 1–2, reversing arms and direction.
Repeat two to four times, each time to a count of eight beats.

Fig. 153

Points to remember:

Keep the arms in a straight line, extending the shoulders in opposite directions.

Possible expected sensations:

Soreness and distension in the shoulders, arms, elbows, wrists, fingers and chest.

Functions:

Relieves stiffness of the shoulders; eases tennis elbow and tenosynovitis of the wrists and fingers; relieves back pain.

5. PUNCHING IN HORSE-RIDING POSITION

Starting position:

Stand with the feet apart at a distance slightly wider than shoulder width, fists at waist.

Movements:

1. Bend the knees as if riding a horse, at the same time punching forward with the left fist, with knuckles facing up. (*Fig. 154*)
2. Open the left fist and turn the palm upward. Return to starting position. (*Fig. 155*)
3–4. The same as 1–2 punching with the right fist.
Repeat two to four times, each time to a count of eight beats.

Points to remember:

Stick out the chest and punch with force.

Possible expected sensations:

Soreness and distension in the arms, wrists, fingers and legs.

Fig. 154

Fig. 155

Functions:

Relieves pain in the neck, shoulders and waist; eases tennis elbow and tenosynovitis of the wrist and fingers.

6. WAIST TWIST

Starting position:

Stand with the feet apart at a distance slightly wider than shoulder width, arms at sides.

Movements:

1. Turn the torso to the left and place the *Hegu* (that part of the hand which lies between thumb and index finger) of the right hand on the left shoulder, palm facing outward. At the same time place the back of the left hand on the lower back. Look at the left shoulder. *(Fig. 156)*

2. Return to starting position.

3–4. The same as 1–2, reversing arms and direction.

Repeat two to four times, each time to a count of eight beats.

Points to remember:

When placing the hand on the shoulder, keep the elbow low, feet flat on the floor. Do the exercise slowly, turning as far as possible.

Possible expected sensations:

Soreness and distension in the neck, shoulders, elbows, wrists and waist.

Functions:

Relieves tennis elbow and pain and stiffness in the shoulders, elbows, waist and back.

Fig. 156

Exercises to Prevent and Cure Functional Disorders of Internal Organs

This set includes massage on acupuncture points (acupressure) as well as movements of the trunk, arms and legs. The exercises improve blood circulation, clean out the main and collateral channels through which vital energy circulates, and enhance the regulatory functions of the nerve secretions. In addition, they strengthen the functioning of the cerebrum and internal organs, heighten metabolism, and help to prevent or relieve disease involving the heart, liver, lungs, kidneys, stomach, intestines and spleen.

1. FACE MASSAGE

Starting position:

Stand with the feet a shoulder-width apart.

Movements:

1. Massage the face with the fingers of both hands in a circular movement from corners of mouth upward to the forehead (*Dicang, Yingxiang, Bitong* and *Qingming* points) and then massage downward with the palms. Repeat eight to sixteen times (one circle = one time). *(Fig. 157)*

2. Massage the face with the palms of both hands from the jaw upward to the temples and then move the palms down behind the ears. (*Baihui* and *Fengchi* points)

Repeat the circular movement eight to sixteen times. *(Fig. 158)*

3. Grasp the left hand with the right, resting both against the upper abdomen. Look ahead. Lick the palate with the tip of

the tongue. Massage the *Shuimian* point, (the one-third part above the second metacarpal bone of the left hand with the right thumb). Then reverse hands and repeat twenty-four to thirty-six times. *(Fig. 159)*

Points to remember:

Close the eyes and concentrate the mind while massaging the *Shuimian* point. When massaging head or face, press palms lightly.

Possible expected sensations:

Warmth on the face; soreness and distension in the *Hequ* point.

Functions:

Relieves nervousness, insomnia, dizziness, palpitation of the heart and stomach and intestinal disorders.

Fig. 157

Fig. 158

Fig. 159

Fig. 160

2. CHEST AND ABDOMINAL MASSAGE

Starting position:

Stand with feet apart at a distance slightly wider than a shoulder width. Place the hands on the upper abdomen with the left palm on the back of the right hand. (*Fig. 160*)

Movements:

1. Massage the upper abdomen in small circular movement eight times.
2. Enlarge the circles to include the chest area for another eight times.
3. Massage the same area in the opposite direction eight times, using a large circular movement, then eight times using a small circular movement.

Points to remember:

Exert some force. Look straight ahead. Slightly protrude and relax the abdomen.

Possible expected sensations:

Warmth in abdomen; belching followed by feeling of relief.

Functions:

Relieves functional disorders of the stomach and intestines; eases lower back pain.

3. "COMBING HAIR" WHILE TURNING TORSO

Starting position:

Stand with the feet apart at a distance slightly wider than shoulder width.

Movements:

1. Place the right palm on top of the head, fingers pointing front. Bend the left elbow and place the back of the left hand against the lower back. *(Fig. 161)*

2. Move hand backward in a combing motion to the neck, turning the torso to the left at the same time. *(Fig. 162)*

Fig. 161

Fig. 162

Fig. 163

3. Move the right palm upward and across, past the right ear to the left side of the forehead simultaneously turning torso and head to the right. *(Fig. 163)*

4. Return to starting position.

5–8. The same as 1–4, using the other hand.

Repeat two to four times, each time to a count of eight beats.

Points to remember:

Press the palm firmly on the head and exert force while combing. Do the exercise slowly and without stopping.

Possible expected sensations:

A comfortable, relaxed sensation in the head; soreness and distension in the waist.

Functions:

Relieves dizziness, blurred vision, insomnia and palpitation.

4. REVERSE ARM AND KNEE LIFT

Starting position:

Stand straight, feet together, fists at waist.

Movements:

1. Shift weight onto the left leg and push the left arm up palm facing up with fingers pointing to the right. Look at the back of the left hand. Open the right fist and press it down with fingers pointing to the front. At the same time, lift the right knee. *(Fig. 164)*

2. Return to starting position.

3–4. The same as 1–2, reversing arms and legs.

Repeat two to four times, each time to a count of eight beats.

Points to remember:

Keep the torso straight. Stretch the arms as far as possible.

Fig. 164

Possible expected sensations:

Soreness and distension in the neck, shoulders, arms, back, waist and legs.

Functions:

Strengthens the spleen and stomach, improving digestion.

5. BEND AND TWIST

Starting position:

Stand with the feet slightly apart, fists at waist.

Movements:

1. Open the fists and push hands upward with palms facing up, fingers pointing at each other. Look at back of hands. *(Fig. 143)*

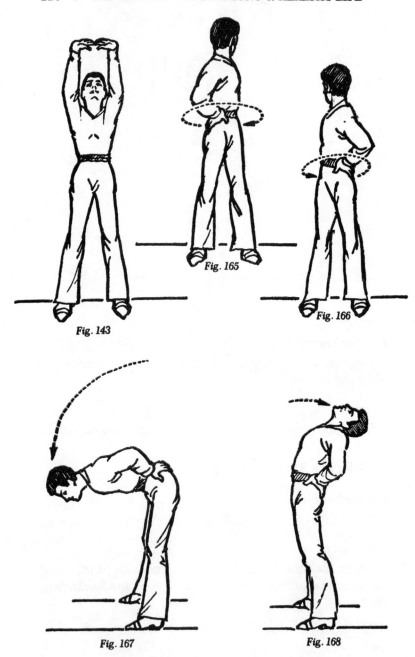

Fig. 143

Fig. 165

Fig. 166

Fig. 167

Fig. 168

2. Drop the hands down and rest the palms on the waist, thumbs pointing front.

3. Turn the torso back to the left, looking backward. *(Fig. 165)*

4. Turn the torso back to the right, looking backward. *(Fig. 166)*

5. Return to position 2.

6. Bend forward 180°. *(Fig. 167)*

7. Bend backward. *(Fig. 168)*

8. Return to starting position.

Repeat two to four times, each time to a count of eight beats.

Points to remember:

Keep the feet flat on the ground. Keep the knees straight while bending forward and backward.

Possible expected sensations:

Soreness and distension in the neck, shoulders, and waist.

Functions:

Relieves pain in the waist and back. Improves kidney deficiencies and strengthens the constitution.

6. STRETCHING ARMS WITH CHEST OUT

Starting position:

Stand with feet slightly apart.

Movements:

1. Cross the forearms at the wrists in front of the body and push up. Then separate the hands with fingers pointing obliquely upward. Look up, lift the heels and inhale deeply. *(Figs. 169–170)*

2. Drop the hands, crossing them in front of the body. Return to starting position. Lower the heels and exhale.

Repeat two to four times, each time to a count of eight beats.

Fig. 169

Fig. 170

Points to remember:

Breathe evenly and naturally. Stretch the forearms upward with force.

Possible expected sensations:

A comfortable sensation in the chest; soreness and distension in the neck and shoulders.

Functions:

Relieves diseases of the respiratory and digestive systems.

III

Twenty Exercises for Treating Diseases and Prolonging Life

"Twenty Exercises for Treating Diseases and Prolonging Life" is a complete set of exercises developed by Mr. Wang Ziping through long years of practice. First published in pamphlet form in 1958, hundreds of thousands of people have been practicing the exercises he introduced.

Partially based on Chinese martial arts ("Wushu"), the twenty exercises have been designed to prevent and treat diseases, build up the physique, delay senility, and prolong life. The exercises embody the principles of unity between respiration and mental regulation (meditation), between the part and the whole, movement and self-massage, motion and stillness, the internal and the external, physical exercise and mental training, and have curative as well as preventive effects upon many diseases and ailments such as lumbago, aching legs, diseases of the cervical vertebra, arthropathy of the shoulders and knees, cardiac disease, hypertension, intestinal and stomach disorders, senile bronchitis, and neurasthenia.

Mr. Wang Ziping (1881–1973) was of the Hui (Muslim) Nationality and was born in Changzhou, Hebei Province—a traditional center of Chinese martial arts. In addition to being a master of martial arts, Wang was an expert in traumatology as well. Having started the practice of *Wushu* at the age of six, Wang could, by the age of fourteen, jump ten feet forward and eight feet backward. He was well versed in all kinds of Chinese martial arts, especially *Chaquan*. Later, he developed a school of his own characterized by equal facility in both attack and defense, smooth, graceful movements, swiftness in motion, stability in stillness and rhythmic coherence in presentation. Known far and wide for his great strength, he was respectfully called "Thousand-Pound Wang." In addition, he had made remarkable attainments in sabreplay, spearplay, swordplay, cudgel fighting, the art of locks and holds, attacking, wrestling, and both soft and hard techniques. In the field of medicine, he developed a school of traumatology—which combines the art of locks and holds with methods used in bone-setting. As can be seen, Wang Ziping enjoyed high esteem in the field of martial arts as well as in traditional Chinese medicine.

Note:

Movements in each exercise should be repeated six to thirty-six times.

1. *SHAN HAI CHAO ZHEN*—Freeing the Mind from Outside Distraction

Starting Position:

Stand upright with the feet a shoulder width apart. Place both hands on abdomen with left hand on top of right hand and both palms facing the body. (*Fig. 171*)

Movements:

1. Inhale slowly and deeply.
2. Exhale slowly. Breathing must be natural and long drawn

Fig. 171

so that the student may gradually learn the abdominal respiration which is referred to in Chinese traditional medicine as *Qi chen dan tian*—drawing the breath down to a point one inch below the navel.

Points to remember:

Relax the entire body, keeping head up with eyes closed naturally, the tip of the tongue touching the upper palate. Free the mind from any outside distraction and concentrate solely on the exercises.

2. *YOU NIAO SHOU SHI*—The Baby Bird Gets His Feed

Starting Position:

Stand upright with the feet apart and the arms hanging naturally.

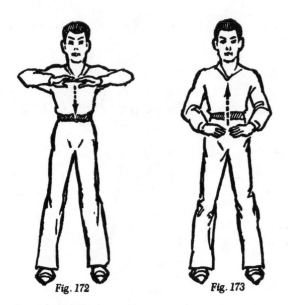

Fig. 172   Fig. 173

Movements:

1. Raise both arms, elbows bent, to chest level, making sure that the palms and forearms are on the same level. Keep the palms facing down.
2. Press the hands vigorously down until the arms are nearly straight. *(Fig. 172)*
3. Return arms to position No. 1. *(Fig. 173)*

Points to remember:

All movements must be slow, with the breathing even and natural. Inhale when lifting the arms and exhale when pressing down. Do not hold your breath. This exercise embodies the unity between mental regulation and respiration and between motion and stillness, with motion as the main factor, and requires the integration of consciousness, motion, and breathing. Exert force with the shoulders when lifting the arms. When pressing the hands down, relax the shoulders as much as possible, exerting force through the palms.

3. *DA PENG YA SU*—The Roc Presses Its Crop

Starting Position:

Stand upright with feet apart and press both hands on the chest, both palms facing inward, with the left hand over the right.

Movements:

1. Make circular movements on the chest and upper abdomen from the upper left to the lower right and around. (*Fig. 174*)

2. Repeat in the opposite direction.

3. Repeat on lower abdomen, with the navel as center, breathing in and out once for each circular movement.

Points to remember:

Keep the head up and look slightly upwards with the torso straight.

Fig. 174

4. *ZUO YOU KAI GONG*—Drawing Bows on Both Sides

Starting Position:

Stand upright with feet apart and put both hands before the eyes with elbows pointing obliquely forward, palms facing outward and fingers slightly bent.

Movements:

1. Separate the hands, slowly clenching them into fists till the fists are on line with the shoulders. Throw out the chest fully. (*Fig. 175*)

Note:

When separating the hands, the movement must be symmetrical and done without lowering the elbows. Exert force slightly through the shoulders, palms and fingers, moving the hands slowly backwards, gradually expanding the chest and pressing the shoulder blades toward each other.

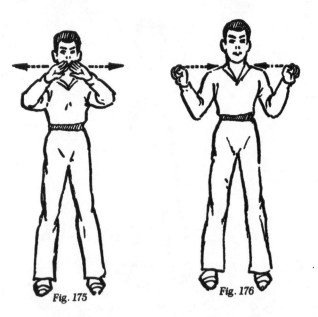

Fig. 175   Fig. 176

2. Keeping the arms bent, open the fists and return to the starting position, drawing the chest inward. (*Fig. 176*)

Points to remember:

Inhale when hands separate and exhale when moving back to the starting position.

5. *BA WANG JU DING*—The Warrior Lifts a Tripod

Starting Position:

Stand upright with the feet a shoulder-width apart. Clench both hands loosely and bend the arms so that the fists are at shoulder level, knuckles facing upwards.

Movements:

1. Open the fists slowly so that the palms face upwards and gently raise both arms with the eyes following the movement of the hands. (*Fig. 177 and 178*)

Fig. 177

Fig. 178

2. Return to the starting position, dropping the hands gently, clenching them into loose fists.

Points to remember:

Inhale when raising hands and exhale when lowering them.

6. *ZHAI XING HUAN DOU*—Pluck Down a Star and Put Another Up

Starting Position:

Stand upright with feet apart, the arms hanging naturally.

Movements: *(Figs. 179 and 180)*

1. Bend the left arm and raise it over the head, with palms facing upward, stretching out fully, rising up slightly onto the balls of the feet. At the same time, press the lower back with

Fig. 179   *Fig. 180*

the back of the right hand. Remember to follow the movement of the left hand with the eyes.

2. Lower the left hand in an arc and place it on the lower back, palm out. At the same time, raise the right hand overhead with palm facing up.

Points to remember:

Inhale when raising the hands and exhale when lowering them.

7. *NEZHA TAN HAI—Nezha** Probes into the Sea

Starting Position:

Stand upright with feet apart, hands at waist, thumbs pointing back.

Fig. 181   Fig. 182

---

*Nezha—a character in Chinese mythology.

Movements:

1. Stretch the neck forward, turning the head down and to the left. Look at a spot on the ground about two meters away from the body, as if trying to gaze at the bottom of the sea. *(Fig. 181)*
2. Return to the starting position.
3. Repeat to the right. *(Fig. 182)*
4. Return to the starting position.

Points to remember:

Inhale when doing 1 and 3, and exhale when returning to the starting position.

8. *XI NIU WANG YUE*—The Rhinoceros Looks Up at the Moon

Starting Position:

Stand upright with feet apart, hands at waist, thumbs pointing back.

Fig. 183   Fig. 184

Movements:

1. Turn the head up and to the left as far as possible, looking in the same direction. *(Fig. 183)*
2. Return to the starting position.
3. Repeat to the right. *(Fig. 184)*
4. Return to the starting position.

Points to remember:

Inhale when turning the head and exhale when returning to the starting position. Exert a little force in the neck when turning. Do not turn the torso or waist when turning and keep the chin drawn slightly in.

9. *FENG BAI HE YE*—Lotus Leaves Sway in Breeze

Starting Position:

Stand upright with feet apart at a distance slightly wider than the shoulders. First rub the hands front and back, then place them on the waist with thumbs forward.

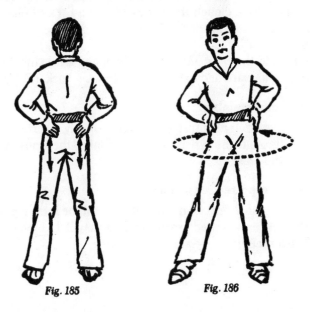

Fig. 185   Fig. 186

Movements:

1. Massage from the lower back down to the coccyx. *(Fig. 185)*
2. Rotate the waist first counter-clockwise, then clockwise, gradually enlarging the circles. *(Fig. 186)*

Points to remember:

Keep the legs straight. Support the lower back with the hands but do not use too much strength. Keep the torso straight.

10. *XIAN REN TUI BEI*—An Immortal Pushes Over a Stone-tablet

Starting Position:

Stand upright with the feet apart at a distance slightly wider than shoulder width, arms hanging naturally.

Movements:

1. Turn the torso to the left and push right hand forward at shoulder level with fingers pointing somewhat upwards. At the same time clench the left hand into a fist and place it on the waist, knuckles down. Turn the head to the left and look back. *(Fig. 187)*
2. Turn to the right and repeat, reversing arms. Inhale when pushing forward and exhale when drawing back. *(Fig. 188)*

Points to remember:

The movements must be executed slowly, exerting a little force through the wrists. Avoid stiffening the arms. Do not move the legs.

Possible expected sensations:

If any pain is felt, do not overdo it; turn the torso gently and slowly. After repeated practice, the pain will disappear gradually over a period of time.

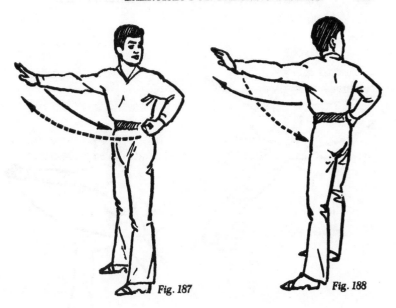

Fig. 187   Fig. 188

11. *ZHANG CHA HUA SHAN*—Thrusting Hands into Mount Hua

Starting Position:

Stand upright with the feet apart at a distance slightly wider than shoulder width, arms hanging naturally.

Movements:

1. Stretch the left arm forward, then turn the palm out and circle it back to waist and turn it into a fist with knuckles down. Thrust the right arm horizontally to the left (as if thrusting with a knife) simultaneously turning the whole body to the left, forming a left "bow step" (bend the left forward leg and straighten the right back leg, with the weight on the forward leg). Keep the right heel flat on the ground. Return to starting position. *(Figs. 189–190)*
2. Repeat to other side.

Fig. 189

Fig. 190

Points to remember:

Keep the eyes on the thrusting hand. Use a little force when thrusting in order to stretch the hip muscles.

12. *BAI MA FENG ZONG*—Parting the White Horse's Mane

Starting Position:

Stand upright with feet apart, cross the hands and place them on the abdomen.

Movements: *(Figs. 191 and 192)*

1. Bend the torso forward, keeping the eyes on the hands. Then straighten up the body, at the same time separating and swinging up the crossed hands until they are over head, stretching out fully.

Fig. 191　　　　Fig. 192

2. Return to the starting position by separating the hands, swinging them down to the sides. Keep the eyes first on the left hand, and then on the right hand during the second repetition.

Points to remember:

Inhale when swinging the hands up and exhale when swinging down.

13. *FENG HUANG SHUN CHI*—The Peacock Trims Its Wings

Starting Position:

Stand upright with the feet apart at a distance slightly wider than shoulder width, arms hanging naturally.

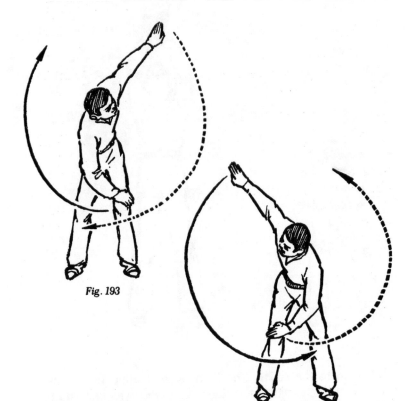

Fig. 193

Fig. 194

Movements:

1. Bend the torso forward with the legs slightly bent. Slowly swing the left hand up along the left side with the head also turned up to the left, eyes on the left hand with the right hand touching the left knee. *(Fig. 193)*
2. Slowly return to starting position.
3. Repeat in the other direction. *(Fig. 194)*

Points to remember:

Inhale when the head turns to the side and exhale when approaching center. Do not exert force when swinging. Do not press with hands when touching the knees.

14. *QIAO JIANG LA ZHUAN*—A Skillful Craftsman Uses His Drill

Starting Position:

Stand upright with feet apart, both fists on waist, knuckles down.

Movements:

1. Turn the feet to the left, pivoting with both feet flat on the floor. Bend at the knees so that the right knee supports left calf. Keep the left fist on the waist. The right fist thrusts forward at shoulder level as the body turns left. *(Fig. 195)*
2. Repeat in opposite direction, reversing arms and legs. *(Fig. 196)*

Points to remember:

Turn slowly and steadily, breathing naturally. This exercise is relatively difficult. Older people may choose to master other exercises first.

Fig. 195

Fig. 196

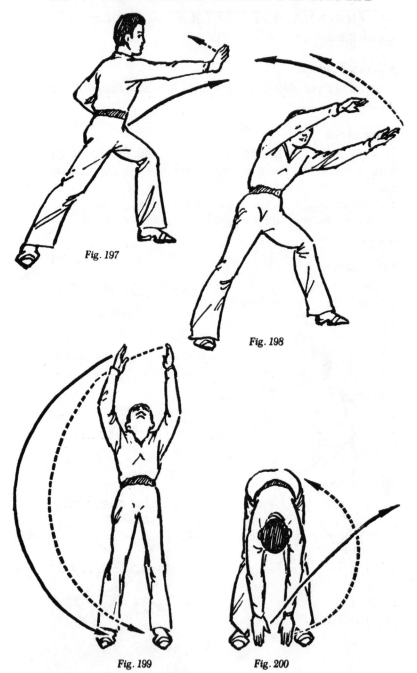

Fig. 197

Fig. 198

Fig. 199

Fig. 200

15. *QING LONG TENG ZHUAN*—The Blue Dragon Soars Up

Starting Position:

Stand upright with the feet apart at a distance slightly wider than shoulder width, hands hanging naturally.

Movements:

1. Clench the left hand into a fist, placing it at the waist, knuckles down. Thrust with the right palm horizontally to the left, simultaneously turning the torso and left foot in the same direction. *(Fig. 197)*
2. Open the left fist and stretch it out to the left. Then swing the parallel arms and torso clockwise, returning to position 1 after completing one circle, and repeat. *(Figs. 198, 199 and 200)*
3. Same as in position 1 to the right, arms reversed.
4. Swing in circle as in position 2.

Points to remember:

Breathe in and out once for each circle. The movement must be executed slowly, keeping the eyes on the hands and the legs straight.

16. *LUO HAN FU HU*—The Arhat Subdues a Tiger

Starting Position:

Stand with the feet wide apart with hands at waist, thumbs pointing back. Keep the torso erect.

Movements:

1. Bend the left leg keeping the right leg straight. *(Fig. 201)*
2. Return to the starting position.
3. Bend the right leg, keeping the left leg straight. *(Fig. 202)*
4. Return to the starting position.

Fig. 201   Fig. 202

Points to remember:

Look forward, keep the torso straight and the feet flat on the ground. When bending either leg, go only so far as you can, without bending too low or too fast. Inhale when bending and exhale when returning to the starting position.

17. *BAI HE ZHUAN XI*—The White Crane Flexes His Knees

Starting Position:

Stand with the feet together, legs slightly bent, torso leaning slightly forward. First massage both knees with the hands, then press the hands on the knees, eyes looking down and forward.

Movements:

1. Rotate the knees in several clockwise circles (*Fig. 203*).
2. Repeat several times in a counterclockwise direction, gradually enlarging the circles.

Points to remember:

Keep the feet flat on the ground, and do not exert force when pressing the knees. Do not keep the head too low. Breathe in and out once for each circular movement.

18. *XING ZHE XIA ZUO*—The Monkey King Takes a Seat

Starting Position:

Stand upright with the feet a shoulder width apart, both fists at the waist side, knuckles down.

Movements:

1. Bend at the knees and squat down as low as possible till the heels touch the buttocks. Open the fists and thrust arms forward, palms facing each other. *(Fig. 204)*
2. Return to the starting position.

Points to remember:

Inhale when squatting and exhale when standing up. Repeat only as often as feels comfortable. Do not squat any lower than feels comfortable. Keep the torso straight and do not lean forward or backward.

Fig. 203   Fig. 204

19. *SI MIAN BAI LIAN*—Swinging the Feet in Four Directions

Starting Position:

Stand upright with the feet together, hands at waist, thumbs pointing back.

Movements:

1. Lift the left knee to hip level and kick out, pointing the toes.
2. Return to the starting position. Lift the right knee and kick out. *(Fig. 205)*
3. Return to the starting position. Kick backwards with the left foot touching the left buttock.
4. Return to the starting position. Kick backwards with the right foot touching the right buttock. *(Fig. 206)*
5. Return to the starting position. Kick up and to the right with the left foot from the knee.
6. Return to the starting position. Kick up and to the left with the right foot. *(Fig. 207)*
7. Return to the starting position. Kick backwards, and up to the left with the left foot.
8. Return to the starting position. Kick backwards, up and to the right with the right foot. *(Fig. 208)*

Note:

The above eight movements can be divided into four sets of two corresponding movements (1 and 2, 3 and 4, 5 and 6, 7 and 8). Each set is to be repeated eight times.

Points to remember:

Inhale when kicking and exhale when returning to starting position. Do not exert too much force. Keep the torso straight and look ahead.

Fig. 205

Fig. 206

Fig. 207

Fig. 208

20. *XIAN ZHONG PAI HUAI*—Sauntering in Fairy Land

Starting Position:

Stand upright with hands at waist.

Movements:

1. Take a step forward with the left foot, heel first.
2. Take a step forward with the right foot, shifting the weight onto it. The left heel should now be raised off the ground. (*Fig. 209*)
3. Take a step back with the right foot, toes touching the ground first, then shift the weight onto the right heel with the left toes coming off the ground.
4. Put the left foot down and take a step forward with the right foot. Then take another step forward with the left foot, toes touching the ground first.
5. Take a step backward with the left foot, toes touching the ground first, shifting weight onto it with the right toes coming off the ground. (*Fig. 210*)

Points to remember:

Each step forward or backward is accompanied by a breath (in and out). Keep the torso straight, looking either straight ahead or down. When lifting the toes or heels off the ground, raise them as far as possible so as to tighten the muscles and tendons of the calves and feet.

Fig. 209

Fig. 210

IV

New *Qigong* Therapy

"*Qigong*" is a part of China's precious cultural heritage and according to written records, has a history of 2000 to 3000 years. "*Qigong*" consists of exercise for relaxation, for training respiration and breath control, and for mental regulation (sometimes referred to as meditation).

Although there are many varied schools of "*Qigong*," what we have chosen for introduction here is the "New *Qigong*," created and written by *Qigong* master and Beijing Art Academy painter, Guo Lin. Guo Lin began to learn *Qigong* and *Wu Qinxi* (Five-Animal-Exercise) in the family at a very early age. Basing herself on 50 years of practice and guided by modern scientific theories, she has created a set of new "*Qigong*" exercises for therapeutic purposes. "New *Qigong*" is a kind of walking exercise which combines motion with stillness and involves different forms and demands. "New *Qigong*" consists of five kinds of regulation exercises: regulation of the mind, posture, respiration, voice production and regulation of combined exercises. The patient can choose those exercises which suit best his particular ailment, case history, constitution and environment.

"New *Qigong*" has also been shown to have a definite effect on chronic diseases. Over the past ten years, Guo Lin has been teaching "*Qigong*" voluntarily in several Beijing parks. According to incomplete statistics, hundreds of patients with chronic diseases, including cancer and cardiovascular disease, have had their symptoms alleviated by practicing "New *Qigong*" with Guo Lin, increasing their life spans and allowing them to return to work.

"New *Qigong* Therapy" combines motion with stillness, with stillness existing in motion and motion residing in stillness. The principles of roundness, softness and extensiveness in movement should be observed in practice. "New *Qigong*" calls for unity of mind, posture and respiration regulation with these three forms complementing each other. Regulation of mind constitutes the heart of the three and is the crux of these exercises. Mind regulation keeps the cerebral cortex in a state of protective inhibition so that the central nervous system may be adjusted and balanced. "New *Qigong* Therapy" involves overall treatment. It can balance the proportions of the body's *Yin* and *Yang*,* keep the arteries, veins and meridians open, bring about the interflow of vital energy and blood, spur the metabolic rate and increase immunity to disease.

To facilitate learning, we have classified the "New *Qigong*" into three levels according to degree of difficulty.

The elementary level consists of five basic exercises, which include nasal respiration coordinated with fixed foot position, slow pacing exercise with lifting-lowering-opening-closing movements, head massage, massage of the *yongquan* point, and cudgel exercise. As these exercises have been formulated in the light of overall treatment, it is advisable for patients of chronic diseases to practice them all. The facts prove that this set of elementary exercises can have a marked effect on various forms of heart disease as well as on other chronic or complicated ailments such as diabetes, gastroptosis, glaucoma, scleroderma and lupus erythematosus. Encouraging results have been achieved in treating cancer with *Qigong*

---

*As mentioned previously, in Chinese medicine *Yin* and *Yang* refer to the two opposing principles in nature. In the body this often specifically refers to body fluids *(Yin)* and vital energy *(Yang)*.

together with surgery and chemotherapy. Of course, in addition to the five basic exercises, cancer patients should also practice medium speed and fast pacing exercises as well as voice production exercises and massage.

Note:

Scientific investigation has not yet been done to ascertain the effectiveness of the independent practice of "*Qigong*". These exercises are complex and can be difficult to learn; improper practice of the more advanced forms could possibly have undesirable side effects. Therefore, it is advisable that the student practice under the supervision of a qualified teacher.

It is also easier if the directions are read to you as you endeavor to execute them. Each exercise is preceded by a preparatory exercise in which you close your eyes and then you do not reopen them until the end of the exercise.

Essentials for New *Qigong* Exercises

Be confident, determined and perseverant.

You must be confident in the effectiveness of the "New *Qigong*" therapy and you must be determined to treat your illness with it. You must be perseverant in its practice.

What distinguishes most "*Qigong*" therapy from other therapies (such as medicinal treatment, acupuncture, massage therapy and magnetic treatment) in which the patient merely passively receives treatment, is that "*Qigong*" therapy relies wholly on the subjective effort and active participation of the patient. Therefore confidence, determination and peseverance are necessary in "*Qigong*" therapy to get good results. Conversely, if the patient is doubtful and lacks perseverance, he will never achieve ideal therapeutic results.

Make better arrangement of your daily life.

Wear light, soft and loose clothing. While doing the exercises, unbuckle your belt, collar and cuffs, loosen your watch strap and wear flat, soft-soled shoes (cloth shoes are best). Abstain from irritant foodstuffs such as hot pepper. Cook well onion and garlic before eating them. Strictly refrain from smoking and drinking. Do not eat or eat only a little before morning exercises. Take a normal meal thirty minutes after exercising. Do not eat excessively before afternoon or evening exercises. Do not do exercises after eating until you have taken an hour's rest. Again, after exercising you should take at least half an hour's rest or engage yourself in some other activity before eating.

In addition, you should keep yourself away from the disturbances of what is referred to in Chinese medicine as the "seven human emotions": anger, joy, brooding, melancholy, sorrow, fear and shock. No sex is allowed during treatment.

Try to achieve roundness, softness and extensiveness in movement.

These three concepts can be described as follows:

ROUNDNESS: Keep the trunk and limbs in round circular postures (or in semi-circular postures) while exercising. Do not be stiff or too erect.

SOFTNESS: Keep the muscles and joints of the neck, trunk and limbs relaxed and soft, not rigid. At the same time, try to be relaxed but not slack.

EXTENSIVENESS: Look straight ahead, then lightly close the eyes, without changing their direction. Concentrate your attention on some point outside the body. (You may concentrate your attention on the "*dantian,*" one to two inches below the navel, only when you have reached a more advanced level.)

Keep in mind the concepts of *Yi* (mind), *Qi* (energy) and *Xing* (form).

Yi refers to all mental activities, including ideology, emotion, consciousness and thinking. *Qi* indicates inner vitality. *Xing* refers to the movements of the body. The exercises are aimed at stimulating vital energy so as to improve blood circulation, unblock the meridians, balance the proportions of body fluids and vital energy, make up for losses of energy and blood, increase immunity to diseases, thus enabling the body to help cure itself. Mental activity plays a key role in bringing forth more vital energy.

The correct practice of mental exercises helps the cerebral cortex to rest in a semi-inhibited state. Only when you concentrate your mind on one point or one object will it be possible to bring forth more vital energy. As vital energy is produced through the regulation of the mind, it is called "mind-regulated energy."

There should be appropriate form to couple with mental activity in breathing exercises, for appropriate form helps bring forth vital energy and enables the vital energy, once obtained, to circle along correct channels. For beginners it takes time to get used to the forms, however, once the forms are mastered, little thought need be given them. At this more advanced stage, the vital energy obtained will help the student perform the forms in a better and faster way. This is called in "*Qigong*" "energy-regulated form."

Preparatory Exercises

1. RELAXED STANDING

Note:

This is the basic form for starting movements of all forms in New "*Qigong*" therapy.

Points to Remember:

In general, this form of exercise calls for tranquility and the exclusion from the mind of all distracting thoughts. It is also required that all parts of the limbs and body be kept natural, neither tense nor slack. In short, keep the mind, limbs and body relaxed, calm and natural.

Method:

1. Stand with the feet a shoulder-width apart, knees slightly bent without their caps exceeding toes. Keep both knees and hips relaxed with the weight of the body centered around *dantian.** (Fig. 211)

2. Look straight ahead; then close the eyes gently without changing the direction of the eyes. This will help to relax the practitioner.

3. Touch the hard palate with the tip of the tongue. Close the lips together gently and slightly.

4. Keep the head upright, bending neither forward nor backward, slanting neither to the right or the left. Otherwise, the

---

**Dantian*, also called *Qihai* in this book, refers to a point located one inch to one and a half inches below the navel.

neck will become stiff and uncomfortable. The neck muscles should not be tense.

5. Keep the shoulders down and elbows lowered, armpits exposed and wrists relaxed. The joints of the wrists, elbows and shoulders should be relaxed; there should always be some space under the armpits so as to ensure smooth circulation of energy and blood.

6. Hold the chest slightly in without bending the back. In this way the spine may be kept straight and relaxed.

7. Do not protrude the lower abdomen. Hold it slightly in without forcing it. That is to say that the abdomen is drawn in as a result of mental activity. Otherwise, side effects will ensue.

8. Relax the lower back. If the lower back is not relaxed, *qi* (energy) will not reach *dantian* (a point below the navel). Only after the lower back is relaxed, can the energy sink down. Squatting and rolling cudgel exercises are particularly conducive to the relaxation of the lower back. These exercises will be examined later.

9. Contract the anus and withdraw the buttocks as if stopping a bowel movement. Do not protrude the buttocks as this would break the state of tranquility and relaxation of the body.

10. After the body is relaxed and the mind concentrated and at ease, knock the upper teeth against the lower teeth lightly thirty-six times. Then do a rinsing motion with the tongue and cheeks. When saliva is produced, swallow it in three gulps and imagine it reaching the middle *dantian* (one and one-half inches below the navel). Knocking the teeth helps to strengthen the teeth, and prevent dental diseases. Swallowing saliva aids digestion, reduces internal heat and fever, and increases the body's immunity to disease. Cancer patients should do this exercise more often.

11. As mentioned before, the key link in attaining good results from "*Qigong*" is to keep the mind at ease, that is, to get rid of various distracting thoughts from the mind.

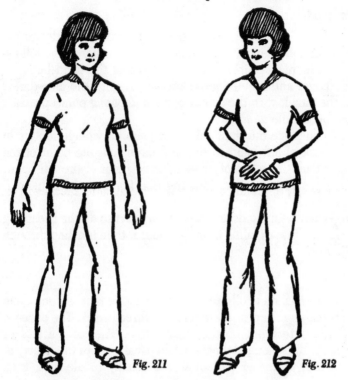

Fig. 211   Fig. 212

2. THREE CYCLES OF BREATHING

This is an exercise of respiration regulation. Breathing in a prescribed manner three times in succession will set up a conditioned reflex in the respiratory nerve center, helping to bring about gradual inhibition of the cerebrum so that the brain can get rest and regulation. So, the "three cycles of breathing" is in itself a kind of exercise and should be done seriously at all stages.

Starting position:

Stand in the relaxed standing position.

Method:

1) Move both hands slowly and gently from the sides to the front of abdomen with one hand over the other in the following fashion: Place the *hukou* (the part of the hand between forefinger and thumb) of the left hand (right hand for women) at the navel, with the center of palm (*laogong* point) pressing on the middle *dantian*.

2) Then place the right palm (left palm for women) on top of the back of left hand so that the inner *laogong* point of the right hand is on top of outer *laogong* point of the left hand. This posture is called "holding *dantian* with both hands." *(Fig. 212)*

3) When both hands are in position, start to do the breathing exercise, first exhaling from the mouth, then inhaling through the nose.

Note:

One exhalation followed by an inhalation is called one cycle of breathing. Repeat three times or three cycles. The purpose of this is to build up the constitution. Therefore a patient weak with prolonged illness would usually adopt this practice. However, a cancer patient would usually inhale first, then exhale.

Points to Remember:

Breathe gently and slowly, steadily and deeply. Never try to take a deep breath with undue force. Keep your waist, hips and knees relaxed during exhalation, squatting slightly. The height and speed at which you squat depends on the nature of disease. Hypertension patients should squat lower and slower than hypotension patients. If the patient's blood pressure is excessively low, he might not squat down at all, merely relaxing the lower back, hips and knees.

When inhaling, do not raise the torso. Keep it in the same position as when you exhale. Otherwise, you will feel short of breath. Only raise the torso after completing inhalation. Also, remember to breathe naturally. By natural breathing we mean breathing without conscious direction. In conversation, people never pay attention to their breathing, although they are breathing all the time.

There also exists the question of speed when raising the torso. This speed depends on the nature of the patient's disease. In general, hypertension patients should raise their torsos faster than hypotension patients. Breathing and form both have the function of regulation. The speed of lowering or raising the torso regulates the function of all parts of the body.

Note:

"Breathing" hereafter refers to exhalation through the mouth followed by inhalation through the nose.

3. THREE ROUNDS OF COVERING AND UNCOVERING MIDDLE *DANTIAN.*

Starting position:

Continued from Three cycles of breathing.

Method:

1) After the last breath, move both hands away from abdomen towards sides so that the backs of hands face each other, fingers together.

2) When the hands have reached shoulder width, turn them so that the palms face each other and slowly move them together towards the middle *dantian.* This is called "covering."

3) Before the hands touch, turn them over again, making the backs of the hands face each other. Repeat two more times. *(Figs. 213 and 214)*

This can be practiced at any point during exercises.

Note:

Middle *dantian* means a point one and one-half inches below the navel or the *qihai* point, upon which you should concentrate your mind in doing preparatory or main exer-

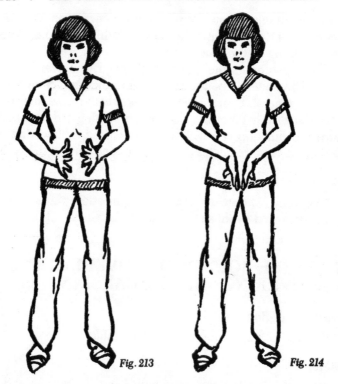

Fig. 213   Fig. 214

cises. Draw vital energy into this point in concluding exercise as well. This is termed "restoration of vital energy," that is, the storing of valuable vital energy into the *dantian* so as to energize the entire body. The inner *laogong* is located at the center of palm while outer *laogong* is at the back of the hand.

Functions:

The exercise of covering and uncovering *dantian* helps strengthen the *laogong* points, stimulate the heart, keep the kidneys fit, alleviate fever and resist chill and regulate the relation between body fluids and energy. It is also fairly effective in the prevention and cure of heart disease, hypertension, fever, arthritis and tonsillitis. It can even be effective in the prevention and cure of cancer, lupus erythematosus and other difficult and complicated ailments.

Elementary Level
Five Basic Exercises

Note:

Do not forget to precede each exercise with "relaxed standing" (Preparatory Exercise 1.).

1. NASAL RESPIRATION COORDINATED WITH FIXED FOOT POSITION.

The purpose of this exercise is to inhale great volumes of fresh air to meet the needs of the internal organs, hence improving their functioning and the body's resistance to disease. The difference between nasal respiration and breathing lies in the fact that during nasal respiration the practitioner is to inhale and exhale through the nose with a sound so slight that it can not be heard by others. The inhalations and exhalations are of short duration and are coordinated with the body's movements. To do nasal respiration, first briefly inhale twice (that is, inhalation, and inhalation again), then exhale immediately afterward. The breathing action becomes inhalation-inhalation-exhalation.

Function:

This exercise helps prevent and cure colds and inflammation.

Note:

It can only be practiced in the early morning and where fresh air is available. It is not advisable to do this exercise at other times (such as after lunch or dinner).

Fig. 215   Fig. 216

A. FIXED LEFT FOOT POSITION:

Starting Position:

After you have done the three cycles of breathing (Preparatory Exercise 2) and the last round of covering and uncovering middle *dantian* (Preparatory Exercise 3), place your hands at the sides of your body.

Method:

1. Shift the weight onto your right foot. Relax the left leg and move it one step forward, heel on the ground, toes up. Begin inhalation.

2) Bend the right leg and place the left foot flat on the ground. Complete the two inhalations.

3) Turn the head, neck and torso slightly to the left with the body leaning slightly forward. Hold in the lower abdomen naturally.

4) Swing the right hand gently to three inches in front of the middle *dantian,* but do not place the hand on the body. At the same time, swing the left hand naturally and gently alongside the lower left hip. *(Fig. 215)*

5) Raise the right heel off the ground, and turn the torso to the right. Swing the left hand to the front of *dantian* and the right hand to the right hip. During this time, perform the exhalation action. *(Fig. 216)* Repeat nine times.

6) Withdraw the right foot to the original position and stand relaxed and calm. Then perform three rounds of covering and uncovering middle *dantian* and three cycles of breathing. (Preparatory Exercises 3 & 2)

Note:

In performing this exercise, try to keep the feet in the same position. Although the body moves repeatedly forward and backward, leftward and rightward, it never moves away from the starting place. Keep joints, lower back and hips relaxed.

B. FIXED RIGHT FOOT POSITION:

Method:

Repeat the above movements nine times, reversing right and left.

C. CONCLUDING EXERCISE:

Method:

1) Withdraw the left foot to the original position and stand relaxed and calm.

2) Perform three rounds of covering and uncovering middle *dantian,* and three cycles of breathing. (Preparatory Exercises 3 & 2) Remove the tip of the tongue from the hard palate. Divert your mind from *dantian.* Open the eyes slowly and move about slowly.

Note:

Nasal respiration is generally practiced in the above manner. But the following three forms of exercises may be adopted in accordance with different conditions.

D. FAST FORM

Method:

Move about faster than during normal performance of the exercise. This form suits best patients with bronchitis, fast erythrocyte sedimentation rate, thrombocytopenia, and hypotension. It does not suit patients with heart disease and hypertension.

E. SLOW FORM

Method:

Move about and breathe slower than during normal practice. The rest of the exercise is the same as that of nasal respiration. This slow form is suitable for patients with hypertension, heart disease and hepatitis.

F. *SHENYU* FORM

Method:

Press the outer *laogong* of both hands (back of hands) against *shenyu* points on the lower back while moving. *(Fig. 217)* This form also can be practiced either fast or slow.

Note:

There is a slight difference between the slow *shenyu* form and the above slow form: when the left foot is in front with toes up, relax the body, lower back and hips. Lean slightly left *(Fig. 218)* first, then shift the lower back and hips gradually to the right *(Fig. 219)*, finally facing forward. The breathing is

Fig. 217   Fig. 218   Fig. 219

done as follows: inhalation and inhalation again when the left toes are up. When the left foot is placed flat on the ground and the body turns to the right, begin to exhale. The inhalation should be done slowly and exhalation even more slowly. After the exhalation is done and the body returns to its original posture, facing forward, breathe naturally. Refrain from holding the breath. In other words, the procedure is inhalation-inhalation-exhalation-pause. Then inhalation-inhalation-exhalation-pause again. Repeat the process nine times. Finally, perform three rounds of covering and uncovering *dantian*, three cycles of nasal respiration, return to the relaxed standing position and conclude. This form is good for gynecological, urinary, heart and kidney ailments, and lupus erythematosus.

2a. EXERCISE OF RELAXATION AND TRANQUILLITY COORDINATED WITH LIFTING-LOWERING-OPENING-CLOSING

Note:

This is a highly potent exercise and may be practiced either independently or as a warming-up exercise for 2b.

Starting position:

Stand relaxed and calm. Then perform three cycles of breathing and three rounds of covering and uncovering middle *dantian.*

A. LIFTING FORM

Note:

Which foot should move forward first depends on the patient's ailment. We start on the right foot for the purpose of demonstration.

Method:

1) Shift weight onto the left leg. Take a step forward with the right foot toes touching the ground first.
2) At the same time, both hands move from the sides towards middle *dantian. (Fig. 220)*
3) Before the middle fingers touch each other, lift both hands slowly up along the central line *(ren mai)* of abdomen and chest. *(Fig. 221)*

Points to Remember:

In lifting the arms, the wrists and elbows should be raised on the strength of the hands. However, hypertension patients should let the hands dangle at the wrists with the inner *laogong* (center of palm) pointing down. Also, do not lift the hands too fast, as this will cause vital energy and blood to shoot up. When the hands are raised, the body should be

Fig. 221

Fig. 220

Fig. 222

shifted slightly forward with the weight on the front leg, and the heel of the rear leg off the ground. But do not bend the body forward. Hold the shoulders down.

4) When the hands are lifted from middle *dantian* to *shanzhong* (a point in front of the chest), change the position of the hands so that the fingers point up and the palms face each other.

5) When the hands reach upper *dantian* (*yintang* point, between the eyebrows), both palms face each other. (*Fig. 222*)

6) Turn palms out in preparation for the next step (for patient of hypotension lift hands slowly with palms up and unfolded, so as to guide the blood upward).

B. OPENING FORM

Starting Position:

Continued from the last form.

Method:

1) Turn hands outward at *yintang* point with outer *laogong* (backs of hands) facing each other.
2) Separate hands in opposite directions, turning palms down. (*Fig. 223*)
3) At the same time, the torso bends slightly backward. Shift weight onto the rear leg. Lift the heel of the front leg off the ground.

Note:

Patients with heart and liver diseases should not separate the hands so far. Do not use force.

C. CLOSING FORM

Starting Position:

Continued from the last form.

Method:

1) When the first two forms are completed, slowly turn the wrists so that the palms face each other, fingers pointing upward. Place the heel of the front leg on the ground while turning palms. (*Fig. 224*)
2) Move both hands slowly towards the front of *yintang* point. At the same time, move the body forward and shift weight onto the front leg, with the heel of the rear foot coming off the ground.
3) When the hands reach *yintang*, the palms face each other with the middle fingers almost touching one another. (*Fig. 225*)

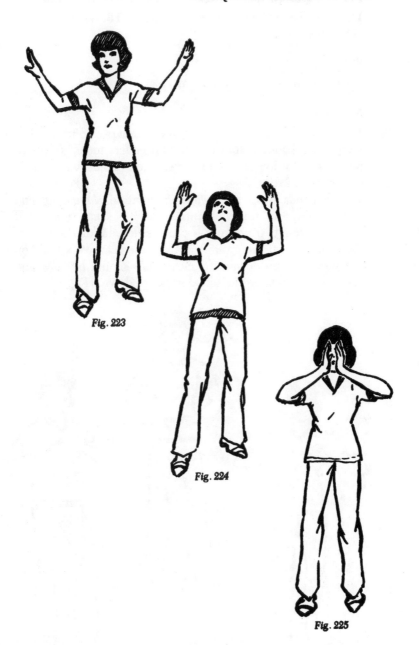

Fig. 223

Fig. 224

Fig. 225

D. LOWERING FORM (FOR PATIENTS WITH HYPERTENSION)

Starting Position:

Continued from the last form.

Method:

1) When both hands meet in front of *yintang* point, start to lower both hands before the middle fingers touch. (Usually, patients with hypertension lower their hands with palms down.) *(Fig. 226)*

2) The hands drop from *yintang* point to *shanzhong* and further down to middle *dantian*. At the same time, shift weight gradually from front leg to rear leg, lifting the heel of the front foot off the ground, placing the rear foot wholly on the ground. The downward movement should be slow and relaxed to help keep the blood pressure down. *(Fig. 227)*

Fig. 227

Fig. 226

Fig. 228

3) When the hands reach middle *dantian,* continue to lower them to the sides of the thighs. Then move both hands up again past middle *dantian.* In lifting the hands, keep the palms towards the body with fingers pointing downward.

4) When the hands reach *shanzhong,* turn palms down with two middle fingers touching one another and drop the hands again. Begin to squat down as the hands drop. *(Fig. 228)*

5) As you squat, keep the torso at right angles to the ground. Do not bend torso forward or backward. So long as you relax the lower back, this can be attained.

6) Following the downward movement of the hands, the body gradually squats down until the thigh of the front leg is parallel to the ground and the hands are at knee level. *(Fig. 229)* (Beginners should not force themselves to squat all the way.)

7) Open and close both hands. *(Figs. 230 and 231)* Then get ready to return to starting position (see F).

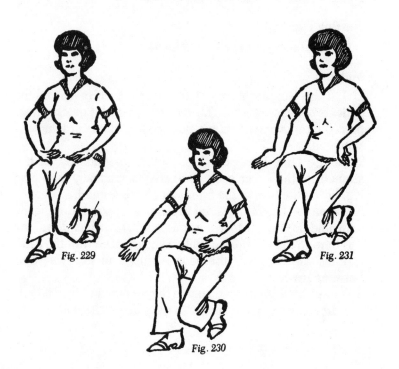

Fig. 229

Fig. 230

Fig. 231

E. LOWERING FORM (FOR PATIENTS WITH HYPOTENSION)

Method:

1) When lowering both hands from *yintang* point, turn the hands with *hukou* forward, palms up.

2) Lower hands along both sides of the face until they reach the outside of the thighs. The fingers should not be held straight, but in an arc. The hands should fall quickly and the palms should be kept upward while squatting down. (The rest of the form is the same as for patients of hypertension.)

Note:

During menstruation, women should not squat down.

F. RETURN TO STARTING POSITION:

Starting Position:

Continued from the last movement.

Method:

1) Lift the hands with wrists and palms down (palms up for patients of hypotension). This may be done a bit quicker than preceding movements (a bit slower for patients of hypotension).

2) At the same time straighten both legs gradually on the strength of the lower back. Shift weight gradually onto rear leg, lifting the heel of the front foot off the ground.

3) When the hands are raised to *shanzhong* point, turn hands with middle fingers touching one another, palms down. At this time straighten the legs fully. Synchronized with the palm turning, the weight of the body is shifted to somewhere in between the legs.

4) Lower both hands gradually to the front of middle *dantian*, and drop them down naturally to the sides of the body.

Note:

A lifting form, an opening form, a closing form, a lowering form and returning form constitute one round. You should perform four rounds, changing directions after each round to relax the waist and hips after each round and stretch a bit.

The direction should be changed in the following way: The direction for the first round is determined by the needs of the slow pacing exercise (2b) which follows. If you intend to start your slow pacing to the east, you should stand facing west to start the lifting-lowering-opening-closing exercise, that is, choose the opposite direction of the slow pace exercise. When you complete the four rounds of lifting-lowering-opening-closing exercise, begun facing west, you will end up facing east.

The first round is usually done facing towards west. Then face south and do the second round. For instance, if the left foot is in front, shift weight onto the rear leg (right leg). The front foot (left foot) is kept relaxed. Its toes turn 90° to the left with the heel as axis. Then shift weight forward onto the front foot (left foot). At the same time, relax the rear foot (right foot), raise it and place it a foot away from the left heel. Now you are facing south and can start the second round.

After the second round is completed, face north as follows: Before the body turns, shift weight onto the rear leg (right leg). Relax left leg and draw it back behind the right heel. Make an about turn in two steps as follows: First step: move left heel inward to form a 90° angle with the right heel, turning on the ball of the left foot. Pause for a while. Move right heel outward 90°, turning on the ball of the right foot. Now you face east. Second step: the left foot moves 90° to the left, turning on the heel. Then, relax the right foot. Raise the right foot and place it a foot away from the left heel (with the left foot in front). Now you are facing north and ready for the third round.

After the third round, face east in this manner: While turning the body, shift weight onto the left leg. Relax the right leg.

Move the right heel inward to form a 90° angle with the left heel, turning on the ball of the right foot. Shift weight immediately onto the right foot. The left foot takes an empty step (Lift the heel off the ground). Then keep left foot relaxed and move it a step forward (the left foot is still in front). Now you are facing east, ready for the fourth round.

It can be seen that you change directions three times in doing four rounds: west-south-north-east. After the completion of four rounds you can start the slow pacing exercise, which together form the 2nd basic exercise of "New *Qigong*."

2b. SLOW PACING EXERCISE

Note:

This exercise constitutes the main section of the elementary level exercises. It embodies most conspicuously the concept of the combination of motion with stillness. In doing this exercise, the regulation of posture is of course important, but what is more important is the regulation of the mind. If you cannot concentrate in doing this exercise, there will be little therapeutic effects even if your movements are graceful. In fact there are some patients whose movements are not ideal who can get good therapeutic results because they can concentrate. Of course, it is most ideal to have perfect regulation of both mind and body.

The exercise of lifting-lowering-opening-closing serves as a warm-up for this exercise. You may also skip the lifting-lowering-opening-closing exercise. You may instead start the slow pacing exercise after performing relaxed standing followed by "three cycles of breathing" and three rounds of "covering and uncovering middle *dantian*". (Preparatory exercises 1, 2, & 3)

Starting Position:

If, for instance, the left foot is in front, move the left foot a step forward placing the heel on the ground first. This move-

Fig. 232

ment is intended to regulate the function of the inner and outer *qiao* arteries. Therefore you should never neglect this minor movement. *(Fig. 232)*

Method:

1) After the left foot is placed wholly on the ground, the right foot takes an empty step (Lift heel off the ground). At the same time, the body turns to the right with the waist as pivot, bringing along the torso, neck and head so as to allow full play to the arteries and veins of the head and *tianzhu* point (a point at the back of the neck).

Note:

You cannot turn easily unless the muscles are relaxed. Otherwise, you will feel discomfort in the neck and head.

2) Simultaneously, the left hand swings forward to the front of middle *dantian*, fingers slightly bent, not stiff. At the same time, the right hand swings over to the right hip. Keep the right hand a bit lower than the left hand. (*Fig. 233*)

Note:

The swinging of the hands should be done in accordance with the principle of roundness, softness and extensiveness with the wrists and elbows relaxed so that the movements gradually take on an arc shape.

3) Shift weight onto the left foot and move the right foot a step forward with the heel on the ground first. Then slowly put the right foot fully on the ground. At the same time, the left foot takes an empty step. While putting the right foot fully on the ground, shift the weight onto the right foot and, turn the body forward. At this time, turn the entire body to the left and swing both hands: the right hand swings to the front of

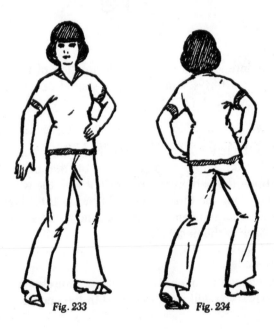

Fig. 233   Fig. 234

middle *dantian,* and the left hand swings to the side of the left hip at a height lower than the right hand. *(Fig. 234)*

4) Continue on in this manner repeating from starting position.

5) Continue walking in this fashion in a circle for half an hour.

Note:

After this exercise, you must perform a concluding exercise. If you are pressed for time, you may shorten the duration of the pacing exercise to twenty minutes and set aside ten minutes for the concluding exercise, or else you cannot amass vital energy into the body and will not be able to build up your strength. On the contrary, you may very well suffer from debility.

CONCLUDING EXERCISES FOR 2a AND 2b

Function:

This exercise serves to amass all the vital energy produced through exercises 2a plus 2b. In this exercise, inner vitality in the channels is guided to *qihai* point (that is middle *dantian)* of the *ren mai* (ren artery). The vital energy goes through the *ren mai* and returns to its due place through the circuits of *ren mai* and *dumai.* Therefore, keep your mind fixed on middle *dantian* during the entire concluding exercise.

A. ATTENTION TRANSITION

Method:

1) Turn your mind to middle *dantian.* This transition of attention is completed with the help of three standing forms of lifting-lowering-opening-closing. This standing form of lifting-lowering-opening-closing is basically performed in the same way as the previously mentioned lifting-lowering-opening-closing exercise. The only difference is that you do not squat down. *(Figs. 235–238)*

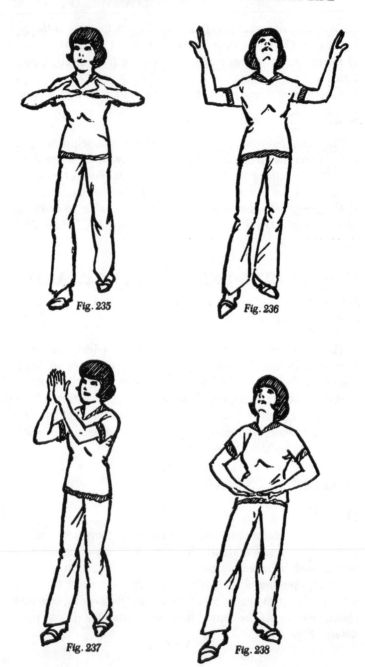

Fig. 235

Fig. 236

Fig. 237

Fig. 238

2) When the lowering movement is completed, shift the weight onto the rear leg and keep your body in a standing position.

3) Slowly drop your hands to middle *dantian.* These movements will help you switch your mind back to middle *dantian.*

B. PLAYING WITH A BALL

Function:

The purpose of this movement is to aid you in your efforts to turn your mind to middle *dantian.* This is not easy for beginners unless they have practiced for quite a long time. The ball-playing movements have been introduced as a means of regulation to help concentrate the mind.

Method:

1) Place both hands about half a foot away from middle *dantian* with palms facing each other one upward, the other downward. (*Fig. 239*)

Fig. 239

2) Imagine you are holding a helium balloon with a diameter of around eight inches. The balloon will change shape if you press it too hard, but if you hold it loosely it will fly away. Therefore you have to hold it with such strength that the ball will neither change form nor fly away.

3) Keep the whole body relaxed, particularly wrists, waist and knees. As you will lift or drop the wrists in rubbing the ball, you should not keep the wrists stiff. Do not make circular movements with shoulders and elbows only.

4) In doing this exercise, both legs will take empty steps in turn and you will have to shift your weight continuously forward or backward.

5) You may rub the ball right in front of your body for a while, at the left side of your body for a while and at the right side of your body for a while. In this way, you can keep your waist, legs and other parts of the body in a soft and relaxed state.

Note:

What deserves your attention most is the steady concentration of your mind on middle *dantian* and not on the ball, that is, do not think of the ball, still less look at it.

C. RELEASE THE BALL

Note:

This has been designed so as not to disperse the vital energy or divert your mind to the hands or the "ball." Again, make sure that you keep your mind on middle *dantian.*

Method:

1) Turn the hands with palms up as if you were holding the ball on the palms.

2) Then slowly lift the hands from middle *dantian* to shan-zhong point *(Fig. 240)* and "release." *(Fig. 241)* When releasing the ball, both hands give a light upward push, moving the hands to a higher position.

3) Perform "release" a second and third time moving hands to

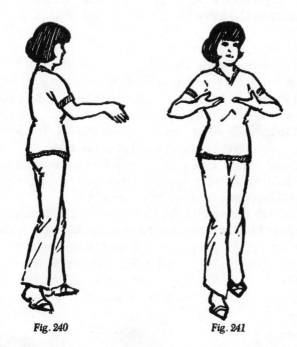

Fig. 240   Fig. 241

a higher position with each push. The position of the hands is now somewhere near upper *dantian*. Move the body a bit forward. By this time, the ball is no longer in your hands. That is to say, you have let the ball go. (Do not let your mind drift away with the ball.)

4) After the ball is gone, turn the hands gradually so that the fingers point up, palms facing inward.

5) Steadily lower the hands down to the front of middle *dantian*.

D. KNEADING THE STOMACH

Function:

The purpose of kneading the stomach is to continue to focus your attention on middle *dantian*. In this manner the vital energy produced will return to its due place and will not stagnate in the limbs.

Method:

1) When the hands which have just set the ball free drop down to middle *dantian*, shift weight onto the front leg.

2) Lift the rear leg forward and land it to the side of the front leg so that you can stand relaxed and calm.

3) Place hands gently on middle *dantian* with the *laogong* point of one hand overlapping that of the other.

4) Slowly make nine circles, each one larger than the one before. *(Fig. 242)* The last circle should not go higher than the *shanzhong* point or lower than the pubis.

5) After the completion of the ninth round, switch position of hands in front of *shanzhong* point *(Fig. 243)*.

6) Circle nine times in the opposite direction, with the circles getting progressively smaller. For the last circle, the hands move around middle *dantian*. After the ninth circle, the hands stop naturally at the middle *dantian*.

Fig. 242   Fig. 243   Fig. 244

Note:

By kneading abdomen, we mean that you are moving your hands outside your clothes as if you were kneading the abdomen. But you are not really pressing your hands against the abdomen and actually kneading, still less are you kneading the abdomen with force. Again, remember to fix your mind on *dantian.*

E. THREE CYCLES OF BREATHING: (PERFORM AFTER KNEADING THE ABDOMEN.)

The method is the same as in the preparatory exercise. But the function is to keep vitality in middle *dantian* and help your mind steadily return to normal state.

F. RECOVERY OF ENERGY (PERFORM AFTER COMPLETING "E".)

Method:

1) Lift hands and elbows to upper *dantian* as in lifting form. Separate the hands in opposite directions over upper *dantian* to shoulder-width with palms in towards the face.

2) Gently and loosely clench both fists with thumbs resting on the forefinger. Tap lightly the inner *loagong* point with the tip of middle finger so that the remaining energy in the hand will return to middle *dantian* through *xinbaojing* (pericardium channels). *(Fig. 244)*

3) After tapping the *laogong* point, pause, Then slowly stretch the fingers. Tap and stretch in this fashion three times.

4) After you clench your fists and tap the *laogong* point for the third time, keep the fingers loosely bent. Then turn the hands so that the thumbs face each other.

5) Close up both hands over upper *dantian* in empty fists.

6) Stretch out naturally the ten fingers and lower the hands along the central line of chest and abdomen past *shanzhong* point to the front of middle *dantian.* The two hands hang

naturally at the sides of the body, returning to the original posture of relaxed standing. Do not open your eyes immediately.

7) Stand there with the eyes closed for a while (about 3–4 minutes). When you have turned your mind away completely from middle *dantian* open your eyes gradually. Move about a bit in place or walk around slowly.

3. *QIGONG* HEAD MASSAGE

Head massage is one of the five basic elementary exercises. Cranial nerves direct all parts of the body. If cerebral nerves do not function properly, the entire body or parts will not work properly either. It is, therefore, of paramount importance to protect the cerebrum, and help bring forth protective inhibition of the cerebral cortex so that the brain gets enough rest and adjustment. *Qigong* head massage was invented for this purpose. Mastery of this exercise can not only regulate the relationship between body fluids *(yin)* and vital energy *(yang)* caused by illness, but can, in coordination with other exercises, also prevent the advent of imbalance between *yin* and *yang* as well. For instance, massage on *yongquan* point can strengthen the kidneys and enrich the body's fluids, whereas head massage can increase the vital energy. Consequently, massage on *yongquan* point alone without doing massage on the head will cause an increase of fluids and a decrease of energy. If patients of hypertension only practice massage on *yongquan* point and refrain from massage on the head, the maximum pressure may remain high while the minimum pressure may come down. Head massage may also prevent cerebral vascular sclerosis. Clearly, it is vital that this exercise should not be taken lightly.

There are ten places on the head which can be massaged. They are the *yintang* point, *taiyang* points (the temples), ears, eyes, nose, *yamen* point, *tianzhu* point, *fengchi* point, *yifeng* point and *yiming* point. (See *Figs. 262 and 263.*)

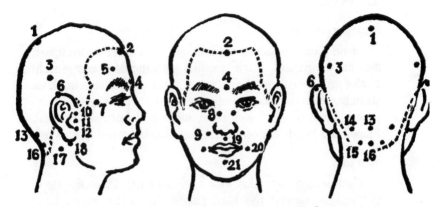

Fig. 262. Points for Massage on Head

1. *baihui*	8. *upper yingxiang*	15. *tianzhu*
2. *shenting*	9. *yingxiang*	16. *yamen*
3. *tianchong*	10. *erman*	17. *yiming*
4. *yintang*	11. *tinggong*	18. *yifeng*
5. *yangbai*	12. *tinghui*	19. *renzhong (shuigou)*
6. *erjian*	13. *fengdi*	20. *dicang*
7. *taiyang*	14. *fengchi*	21. *chengjiang*

Figure 263. Points Around Eyes

1. *zanzhu*
2. *shangming*
3. *sizhukong*
4. *jingming*
5. *tongziliao*
6. *chengqi*

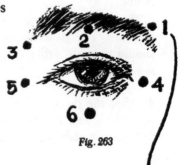

Fig. 263

A. WARM-UP

Starting position:

Sit on a cushioned stool with legs a shoulder-width apart, feet flat on ground, thighs parallel with the floor and at right angles to the calves. Keep torso erect with chest in, back straight, shoulders down, elbows naturally bent, armpits exposed, head erect, lower back, waist and buttocks relaxed. Place both hands flat on thighs with fingers pointing forward.

Method:

1) Look straight ahead. Close eyelids gently. Place the tip of the tongue against the hard palate. Keep the entire body relaxed. Rid your mind of distracting thoughts.

2) Place both hands on middle *dantian*. For males, place the inner *laogong* of the left hand gently on middle *dantian* and that of the right hand on the outer *laogong* of the left hand. For females, reverse hands.

3) When the hands are in correct position, perform three cycles of breathing, first exhaling through the mouth, and then inhaling through the nose. Exhaling once plus inhaling once is considered as one cycle. Repeat three times. Breathe quietly, slowly, steadily, deeply and naturally. Never try to force a steady and deep breath. Otherwise discomfort will ensue. Breathing is practiced in a sitting position, and not in a standing position, you don't have to squat down. But you must relax the waist and lower back.

Note:

The above is the breathing method for patients of ordinary diseases. For patients with tumors and cancer, inhalation should precede exhalation. The rest of the procedure is the same.

4) After the three cycles of breathing, perform three rounds of covering and uncovering middle *dantian* in the same way as it is done in standing position.

Note:

Whenever three cycles of breathing and three rounds of covering and uncovering middle *dantian* are mentioned hereafter, perform in the above fashion. No further explanation will be provided.

B. MASSAGE *YINTANG* POINT (*Fig. 262, No. 4*):

Starting Position:

Continued from the three rounds of covering and uncovering middle dantian in the warm-up exercise.

Method:

1) Lift up the hands slowly to *yintang* point (upper *dantian*), with the elbows and arms rising naturally and steadily, fingers together, middle fingers touching each other. (*Fig. 245*) (Patients of hypotension should keep the palms up, while patients of hypertension should keep them down).

Note:

Keep in mind that in the following passages when the lifting of hands is mentioned, the position of the palms—facing up or down—should be decided in accordance with your situation. No further explanation will be made.

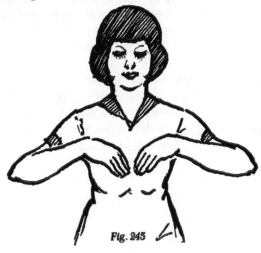

Fig. 245

2) When both hands reach somewhere around *shanzhong* point, raise the fingers naturally upward to *yintang* point. Then straighten the forefingers and middle fingers of both hands and put them together. Bend the other fingers with the thumbs pressing lightly the outside of the ring finger nails; put the pinkies naturally together with the ring fingers. *(Fig. 246)* This position is called "pointing finger."

3) Massage the *yintang* point with the tips of the middle fingers. Keep the middle fingers on the same level, placing them gently on the *yintang* point at the same time. Rub in counter-clockwise circles nine times and then in clockwise circles nine times. *(Fig. 247)*

4) Lightly press the point, exhaling at the same time. Inhale when releasing pressure. Hence press-exhale, release-inhale. Repeat three times.

Note:

Do not rub and press the point with too much force. Do it so gently that you just feel a little touch of the fingers on the point; you must not feel pressure on the point. If too much force is put on the point, results may not be ideal, and you will feel uncomfortable.

Note:

In future whenever the terms "nine counter-clockwise circles and nine clockwise circles" and "three presses and three cycles of breathing" appear it refers to the above sequence of movements. There will not be any further explanation.

5) When you have done the massage on *yintang* point, move the fingers upward to *shenting* point (a point at the middle of the forehead near the edge of the hair). *(Fig. 248)*

6) Tap the forehead with the middle fingers while moving them upward. Then tap the forehead back down to *yintang* point.

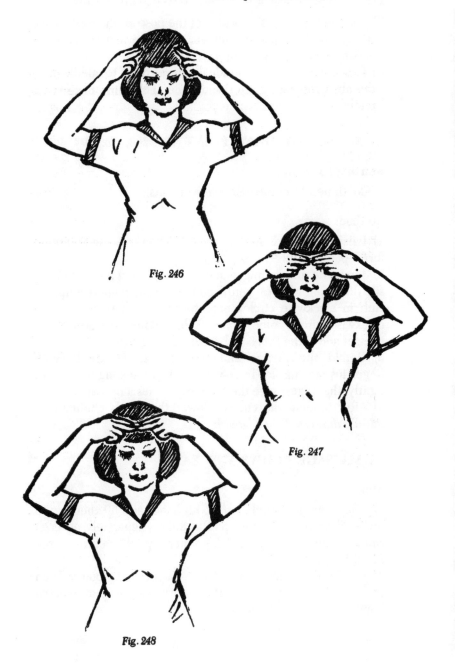

Fig. 246

Fig. 247

Fig. 248

7) Tap both sides of the bridge of the nose all the way downward to *renzhong* point (philtrum, the vertical groove on the median line of the upper lip).

8) Relax both hands and gradually lower them to middle *dantian*. Turn the hands over and raise them upward. Take a breath.

C. MASSAGE *TAIYANG* POINT *(Fig. 262, No. 7):*

Starting Position:

Continued from the above movements.

Method:

1) Raise both hands slowly upward. When reaching *yintang,* form "pointing fingers" position.

2) Move the middle fingers away from *yintang* point in opposite directions and rest gently on the *taiyang* points (temples). Rub in clockwise circles nine times and then in counterclockwise circles nine times. When done, perform three presses and three cycles of breathing. *(Fig. 249)*

3) Unfold the fingers and tap the cheeks gently with fingertips moving slowly downward. Just touching the cheeks lightly, the fingers give the facial capillaries a massage.

4) After tapping the cheeks, lower the hands gradually to middle *dantian*. Take a breath.

D. MASSAGE BROWS AND EARS.

Method:

1) After taking a breath, turn both hands and lift them up to upper *dantian*. Place the middle fingers separately on each *zanzhu* point (a point at the inner tip of eyebrows; see *Fig. 263, No. 1*).

2) Place the thumbs separately on each *taiyang* point. Then the middle fingers stroke the brows, stopping at *taiyang* points. Repeat three times.

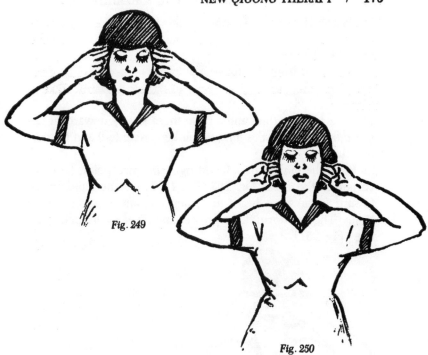

Fig. 249

Fig. 250

3) Connect the thumbs with the pinkies of both hands. Straighten out the forefingers, middle fingers and ring fingers and put them together. Place the forefingers, middle fingers and ring fingers one each on *ermen* *(Fig. 262, No. 10)*, *tinggong (Fig. 262, No. 11;* the point hollows out when you open your mouth) and *tinghui (Fig. 262, No. 12;* this point also hollows out when you open your mouth) with palms forward.

4) Knead each set of points in clockwise circles nine times and in counter-clockwise circles nine times. *(Fig. 250)*

5) Practice three presses and three cycles of breathing. Then, disconnect the thumbs and little fingers. The fingers tap the cheeks gently moving slowly downward to give the capillaries a massage.

6) Finally the hands are lowered to middle *dantian.* Take a breath.

E. MASSAGE THE EYES

Starting Position:

Continued from the above movements.

Method:

1) After turning the hands, raise them slowly upward to upper *dantian*. Place the fingers (pinkies excluded) and thumbs together.

2) Place the pinkies on left and right *jingming* points (at inner corner of the eyes; *Fig. 263, No. 4*). Move the hands in an inward circle nine times and then outwardly also for nine times. Then perform three presses and three cycles of breathing. *(Fig. 251)*

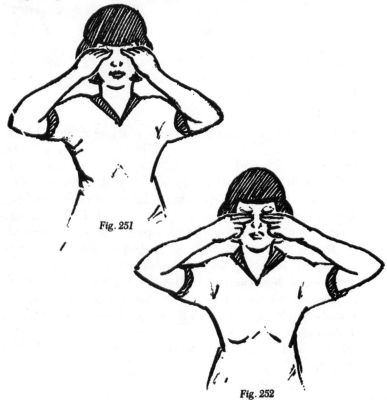

Fig. 251

Fig. 252

3) Move the little fingers gently outward across the closed eyes to *yuwei* (outward corner of the eyes). Then circle the hands at *yuwei* inwardly and outwardly nine times each. Then practice three presses and three cycles of breathing.

4) Unfold the fingers and massage the capillaries of the face. After tapping the face downward, lower the hands to middle *dantian*.

5) Turn hands at middle *dantian* and lift them up to upper *dantian*. Place little fingers on the *chengqi* points (*Fig. 263, No. 6;* below the eyes). Move the little fingers inward on the point and then outward in a circular motion nine times each. Then perform three presses and three cycles of breathing.

6) Place the little fingers on the *yuyao* points (the middle of the eyebrows, right above the pupils). Move the little fingers on the point inward, then outward in a circular motion nine times each. Then perform three presses and three cycles of breathing.

7) Unfold the fingers, tap the cheeks with the finger tips, moving gradually downward. Lower both hands slowly to middle *dantian*. Take a breath.

F. MASSAGE THE SIDES OF THE NOSE

Method:

1) Turn hands and raise steadily upward till upper *dantian*. Change to "pointing fingers position." The pointing fingers move down through the space between the eyebrows, along the sides of the bridge, past upper *yingxiang*, and *yingxiang* points (*Fig. 162, No. 8 and 9*) along the groove between nose and corner of mouth past *dicang* point (*Fig. 162, No. 20*). Repeat three times. (You may repeat several times more if you have a cold.)

2) After massaging the nose, lower the hands slowly down to middle *dantian*. Take a breath. (*Fig. 252*)

G. MASSAGE *YAMEN* POINT (INCLUDING *YANGBAI, LUGU* AND *YAMEN* POINTS)

Starting Position:

Continued from the above movements.

Method:

1) Both hands move from middle *dantian* gradually upward to upper *dantian.* Arrange the fingers as in *Fig. 250.*

2) Place middle fingers on each *yangbai* point (one inch above the eyebrow on line with the pupil). Move the fingers inward and then outward in a circular motion nine times each. Then perform three presses and three cycles of breathing.

3) Move both hands towards *yintang* at the center and unfold the fingers. Stroke the head gently with the palms. At the same time stroke with a little force using the fingertips along the central line of the head up to *baihui* point (the intersection of the line formed between the tips of the ears and the central line on the head).

4) Separate the hands.

Note:

Hypertension patients may join the two middle fingers while patients of hypotension should not. Nor should they move the hands to *baihui* point.

5) Place both hands on the top of the head *(Fig. 253).* The hands circle first in a counterclockwise direction, then clockwise nine times each. After that perform the three presses and three cycles of breathing. (This exercise will be referred to later as "massage on *yangbai* point.")

6) Both hands move from *baihui* point to the *yamen* point (at the back of neck on the central line, that is, right on the groove between the first and second cervical vertebrae). The pointing fingers move on the *yamen* point in a circle (leftward for males; rightward for females) nine times, and then in the opposite direction nine times. When these movements are

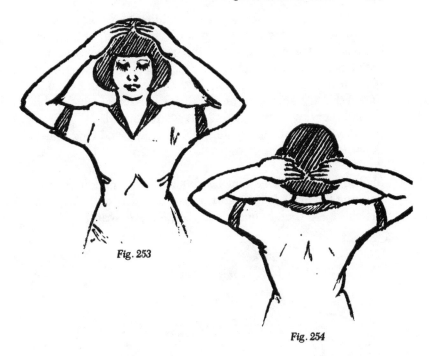

Fig. 253

Fig. 254

completed, perform three presses and three cycles of breathing. *(Fig. 254)*

7) Unfold the fingers and rub the neck with the fingertips, moving them forward and up to the forehead. Then lower the hands to middle *dantian* going past the chest. Take a breath.

H. MASSAGE *TIANZHU* POINT

Starting Position:

Continued from the above movements.

Method:

1) Turn hands and lift both hands gradually from middle *dantian* to *shanzhong* point and turn hands. Lift further to upper *dantian,* and perform "massage on *yangbai* points."

2) Both hands move along the central line of the head backward and downward to *fengfu* point (at upper part of the back of neck, on the central line of the back of the neck and one inch beyond the hairline). Then pinch the muscles starting at *tianzhu* points (*Fig. 262, No. 15;* at the nape; at the outside line of the nape muscles; on the upper horizontal edge of the second cervical vertebrae, somewhere outside of *yamen* point) with thumb, forefinger, middle finger and ring finger down to the bottom of the neck. Repeat three times. (*Fig. 255*)

3) Stroke gently three times with forefingers, middle fingers and ring fingers. Move fingertips past the sides of the neck to the chest and then to middle *dantian.* Take a breath.

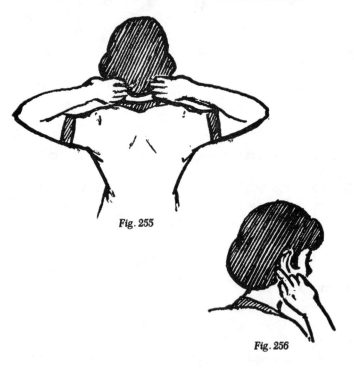

Fig. 255

Fig. 256

I. MASSAGE *FENGCHI* POINT.

Starting Position

Continued from the above movements.

Method:

1) Turn hands. Lift them up slowly to upper *dantian*, and perform finger "massage on *yangbai* points."
2) Move both hands backward and downward to the *fengchi* points (along the central line of the head; *Fig. 262, No. 14*). Move pointing fingers on the *fengchi* points inward, then outward in a circular motion nine times each direction. Then perform three presses and three cycles of breathing.
3) Unfold the fingers. Move fingertips past the sides of neck to the chest and then to middle *dantian.* Take a breath.

J. MASSAGE *YIFENG* AND *YIMING* POINTS

Starting Position:

Continued from the above movements.

Method:

1) Turn hands. Lift both hands up slowly to *yintang* point. Change finger position to form pointing fingers. Place both middle fingers on *yifeng* points (*Fig. 262, No. 18*).
2) Move the fingers on the points forward and then backward in a circular motion for nine times each direction. Then perform three presses and three cycles of breathing. (*Fig. 256*)
3) Place forefingers on *yiming* points (*Fig. 262, No. 17*) and move the fingers on the points in forward and backward circles nine times each direction. This being done, perform three presses and three cycles of breathing.
4) Unfold the fingers and put them together. Move them to the chest past the sides of neck and then to middle *dantian.* Take a breath.

K. RECOVER ENERGY

Starting Position:

Continued from the above movements.

Method:

1) Lift both hands gradually upward along upper *dantian* without touching the head. When the hands reach *baihui* point, the hands touch the head, then move back down while kneading the neck gently sliding past *tianzhu* point to the chest, finally reaching middle *dantian.* Repeat the movements for three times.

2) Conclude by doing three rounds of covering and uncovering middle *dantian* and three cycles of breathing.

Points to Remember:

At the initial stage, you need not regulate your mind while massaging your head. After you master the movements, you may regulate your mind through mind focusing, subject selection, and subject holding in order to get rid of distracting thoughts. (See "Mental Training" at end of chapter) After the massage is completed, you must turn your mind onto middle *dantian* while doing the concluding exercise. When the concluding exercise is done, calm yourself for a minute. When your mind is diverted from middle *dantian* and the tip of the tongue detaches itself from the palate, you may slowly open your eyes and move about as usual.

4. *QIGONG* MASSAGE ON *YONGPUAN* POINT

Function:

Massage on *yongquan* points has very satisfactory therapeutic effects upon such ailments as strained lumbar muscles and weak legs, edema of the lower limbs, and insomnia and giddiness caused by loss of energy and impaired kidney functioning. The kidneys are a source of life. Massage on *yongquan* can build up the kidneys and make the body fluids flow smoothly. Having ample fluids is good for the coordinated functioning of the heart and kidneys and can build up the internal organs, thus helping to prevent and/or cure disease, keep you fit and prolong your life.

A. WARM-UP

Starting Position:

The same as in *Qigong* Head Massage: Sit on a cushioned stool with legs a shoulder-width apart, feet flat on ground, thighs parallel with the floor and at right angles to the calves. Keep torso erect with chest in, back straight, shoulders down, elbows naturally bent, armpits exposed, head erect, lower-back, waist and buttocks relaxed. Place both hands flat on thighs with fingers pointing forward.

Method:

1) When you are in the correct sitting position, look straight ahead. Close eyelids gently. Place the tip of the tongue against the hard palate. Keep the entire body relaxed. Rid your mind of distracting thoughts.

2) Place both hands on middle *dantian.* For males, place the inner *laogong* of the left hand gently on middle *dantian* and that of the right hand on the outer *laogong* of the left hand. For females, reverse hands.

3) When the hands are in correct position, perform three cycles of breathing, first exhaling through the mouth, and then inhaling through the nose. Press the point lightly when exhaling and release the pressure slowly when inhaling. Exhaling once plus inhaling once is considered as one cycle. Repeat three times.

Note:

Breathe quietly, slowly, steadily, deeply and naturally. Never try to force a steady and deep breath. Otherwise discomfort will ensue. Breathing is practiced in a sitting position, and not in a standing position; you don't have to squat down. But you must relax the waist and lower back.

Note:

The above is the breathing method for patients of ordinary diseases. For patients with tumors and cancer, inhalation should precede exhalation. The rest of the procedure is the same.

4) After the three cycles of breathing, perform three rounds of covering and uncovering middle *dantian* in the same way as it is done in standing position.

Note:

Whenever three cycles of breathing and three rounds of covering and uncovering middle dantian are mentioned hereinafter, perform in the above fashion. No further explanation will be provided.

B. MASSAGE ON *YONGQUAN* POINT OF THE LEFT FOOT

Starting position:

Sit on the edge of stool with the left leg bent at the knee and left foot flat on stool. Put the right foot flat on the ground, flexed at the knee at a ninety degree angle.

Method:

1) Place outer *laogong* point of the left hand (the back of the hand) right on the left *shenyu* point of the waist.

Note:

If it is too difficult to put the left hand on *shenyu* point (one and a half inches away from the 14th vertebrae), you may put your hand on the lower abdomen instead with *laogong* (palm) right on the *guanyuan* point (three inches below navel). If your ailment lies in the part of the body cavity below navel, you should not place your hand on the lower abdomen. Instead you may place your hand on the thigh with the fingers together and pointing forward.

2) Place the right hand flat on the left sole with the palm right on *yongquan* point. With *yongquan* point as the center, the hand rubs the sole in circular movements, moving counterclockwise (clockwise for females) gently and slowly seventy times.

3) Perform three cycles of breathing with palm (*laogong* point) right on *yongquan* point (press the point lightly when exhaling, and release the pressure without taking away the hand while inhaling).

4) Move the right hand clockwise for seventy-two circles. Perform three cycles of breathing, then another seventy-two circles counter-clockwise and three cycles of breathing. Perform three rounds of all the above (reversing rubbing directions for women).

5) Put the left leg on the ground, and sit normally. Perform three rounds of covering and uncovering middle *dantian,* and three cycles of breathing.

C. MASSAGE ON *YONGQUAN* POINT OF THE RIGHT FOOT

Starting position:

The same as in the above form, with arms and legs reversed on stool.

Method:

1) After rubbing foot as in previous form, place the right foot on the ground, and perform three rounds of covering and uncovering middle *dantian,* directing your mind to middle *dantian.*

2) Perform three cycles of breathing as done in the concluding exercises.

3) Place both hands slowly on the thighs. Remove the tip of the tongue from the hard palate. After your mind is directed away from middle *dantian*, open your eyes slowly.

Note:

It is best to go to sleep after massaging the *yongquan* points. If you want to take a walk after massage, you must first rest ten minutes. Massage on *yongquan* points is an independent exercise, and should be done only with a ten minute rest after other exercises. One or two hours rest is required between this exercise and massaging points pertaining to vital energy channels such as head massage. During menstruation women should stop practicing this exercise.

Avoid by all means doing this exercise with force, or else you will fail to attain good therapeutic results, and some side effects may ensue such as high blood pressure and insomnia. Such principles in mental exercise as "no staring, no searching and no forcing," "hazy notion and spacious concentration" are also applicable when counting the number of repetitions. As a result, the actual number of repetitions is of no vital importance. You may repeat a bit more or less than seventy-two times. In fact, if you stick to a fixed number, you may cause negative side effects, thus affecting the therapeutic results. All in all, keep relaxed, calm and natural. Refrain from forceful rubbing and overstraining the mind.

5. EXERCISE OF ROTATING A CUDGEL WITH THE WHOLE BODY RELAXED

Function:

This is one of the five basic elementary exercises. Just as the name implies, this exercise was invented to relax the brain and the whole body. It is suited for relaxing muscles, promoting blood circulation, clearing main and collateral channels and eliminating stagnation of energy and blood. Coordinated with the slow pacing exercise and head massage, this exercise may bring about even better curative effects. Moreover, it may prevent and rectify various side effects caused by errors. Therefore practitioners should take it seriously.

Equipment:

It is better to have a cudgel made of Chinese prickly ash, because that kind of wood can help relax muscles and promote circulation. If this type of wood is not available, any other hard wood will also do. A cudgel of eight inches long is most appropriate, but for a well-built person, the cudgel may be a bit longer. It should not exceed nine inches though, and for thin people, it may be a bit shorter, but it should not be shorter than eight inches. The cudgel should be straight, for it is not easy to turn a crooked cudgel. A cudgel with a diameter of one inch is most appropriate. It may be a bit thicker for people with larger hands or thinner for those with smaller hands. Both ends of the cudgel should be convex in shape.

A. WARM-UP

Starting Position:

First perform relaxed standing, holding the middle of the cudgel with the right hand. The thumb touches lightly the tip of middle finger. *(Fig. 257)*

Method:

1) Place *laogong* point of the left hand gently on middle *dantian*. Put the right cudgel-holding hand on the outer *laogong* point of the left hand (the reverse for females). When hands are in the right position, perform three cycles of breathing and three rounds of covering and uncovering middle *dantian*.
2) Hold the cudgel at both ends between the palms. Keeping the cudgel horizontal, rotate it first away from the body, then towards it, using the wrists. It does not matter how many times you rotate the cudgel. Do not let the cudgel go higher or lower than middle *dantian*.

Note:

Hereafter, the "rotating of cudgel in front of middle *dantian*" refers to these movements. It is better to do this exercise at a faster speed to avoid stiffness.

B. ROTATE CUDGEL IN FRONT OF MIDDLE *DANTIAN*

Starting Position:

Continued from the above movements.

Method:

1) Move left foot (or right foot as the case may be) a step forward with toes touching the ground (cancer patients put heel on ground).

2) Following a forward leaning of the torso, the front foot is put wholly on ground and the heel of the rear foot is lifted up. (Rear foot takes empty step while front foot is fully on the ground.)

3) Rotate the cudgel for a while. *(Fig. 258)*

4) The body now returns to its original position, then leans slightly backward.

5) Place the heel of the rear foot on ground and lift the heel of the front foot off the ground. Now front foot takes an empty step while rear foot is fully on the ground. Rotate the cudgel for a while. One forward and one backward movement is considered one round. Repeat four rounds.

6) After four rounds with the left foot in front, move the rear foot (that is the right foot) a step forward. Return to starting position.

7) Stand with the feet a shoulder-width apart. Hold the cudgel in the right hand. Perform one round of covering and uncovering middle *dantian*.

8) Move the right foot a step forward and repeat the previous movements another four times.

9) Move the left foot a step forward and return to starting position.

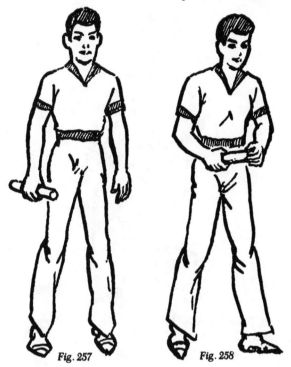

Fig. 257   Fig. 258

10) Stand with feet a shoulder-width apart, with the right hand holding the cudgel. Move both hands forward to the front of middle *dantian*. Perform three rounds of covering and uncovering middle *dantian* and three cycles of breathing.

C. ROTATE CUDGEL SQUATTING

Starting Position:

Continued from the above movements.

Method:

1) Rotate cudgel with both hands. Simultaneously the left foot takes a step forward. Lean the torso forward with weight shifted onto the front leg. Keep lower back relaxed.

Fig. 259

2) The body squats down slowly until the left thigh is parallel to the ground. (The front foot is fully on the ground while rear foot takes an empty step.)

Note:

Beginners may not be able to squat down fully, and should not force themselves. Squat down as far as you can. Gradually you will be able to squat down fully.

3) Hold the cudgel at middle *dantian* level. Rotate the cudgel in front of middle *dantian* for a while. *(Fig. 259)*
4) Raise the torso slowly on the strength of the lower back. When the body is straightened up, place both feet flat on the ground.
5) Relax the front leg, tighten the rear leg, and lean the body slightly backward. When leaning backward, keep the torso straight. After rotating the cudgel, return to original position. Repeat four times.

6) Move the right foot a step forward so that the feet are together (starting position). Hold the cudgel in the right hand. Perform one round of covering and uncovering middle *dantian*.

7) Change foot position by moving the right foot a step forward. Repeat four times all movements done while the left foot was in front.

8) Move the rear foot forward with the right hand holding the cudgel. Place both hands in front of middle *dantian*. Perform three rounds of covering and uncovering middle *dantian* and three cycles of breathing.

D. ROTATE CUDGEL TO THE SIDE

Starting Position:

Continued from the above movements.

Method:

1) The left foot takes a step forward with weight on the left leg. Lift the right heel to form a right empty step.

2) Place the right heel down by the left heel. Gradually shift weight onto the right leg. Then lift the left heel.

3) Turn the body ninety degrees to the right. The left foot turns at the same time with the toes pointing obliquely to the right. Rotate the cudgel for a while.

4) Return to starting position facing forward. Place the left heel on the ground and lift the right heel off ground. Repeat four times.

5) Return to original position and stand erect. Perform one round of covering and uncovering middle *dantian* with the cudgel in the right hand.

6) Change foot position so that the right foot is in front. Repeat the above movements four times, reversing directions. After the body returns to starting position, perform three rounds of covering and uncovering middle *dantian* and three cycles of breathing with cudgel in the right hand.

E. ROTATE CUDGEL AT *BAIHUI* AND *YAMEN* POINTS ON THE HEAD

Starting Position:

Continued from the above movement.

Method:

1) Move the left foot a step forward to form a bow step. Rotate the cudgel in front of middle *dantian* with both hands, lifting the hands slowly while turning the cudgel.

2) Simultaneously shift weight gradually onto the rear leg. Relax the front leg, lifting the heel off the ground. While turning the cudgel, raise the hands to *baihui* point.

3) With the front heel off the ground, move both feet so that they are on the same line, and lean the torso backward.

4) Continue to move the hands to *yamen* point at the back of the neck, cudgel still rolling. Do not bend the torso further backward when you roll the cudgel down to *yamen* point. Keep both feet on the same line with the left foot in an empty step and right foot wholly on the ground. *(Fig. 260)*

5) Roll the cudgel upward in both hands from *yamen* point to *baihui* point. When the cudgel moves past the *baihui* point the left foot takes a half step forward. *(Fig. 261)*

6) Lower the hands slowly down to middle *dantian,* the cudgel still rolling. At the same time, take another bow step, with weight distributed evenly between both legs. Perform four rounds with the left foot in front.

7) Move the rear foot forward so that both feet are on line again. The right hand, holding the cudgel, is put in front. Perform one round of covering and uncovering middle *dantian.*

8) Change position so that the right foot is in front. Repeat the above movements four times.

9) Perform three rounds of covering and uncovering middle *dantian* and three cycles of breathing.

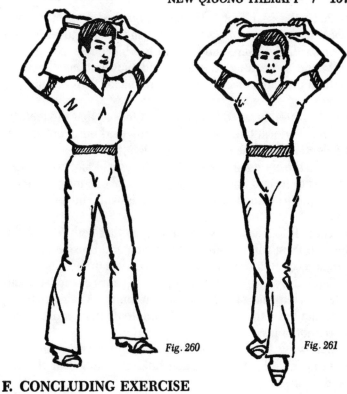

Fig. 260

Fig. 261

F. CONCLUDING EXERCISE

Starting Position:

Continued from the above movements.

Method:

1) Divert your attention from a specific subject to middle *dantian.*

2) Move the left foot a step forward to form a bow step with the cudgel in the right hand. The rear foot takes an empty step with the toes on the ground as the right hand with cudgel in it moves from middle *dantian* slowly upward to *shanzhong* point along the *ren* artery.

3) Place the rear foot flatly on the ground when the hand reaches *baihui* point. The right hand then moves slowly downward, rightward and forward in a half circle.

4) At the same time, the left hand moves along the same route in the same manner as the right hand. Perform this four rounds.

5) Take a step forward with the right foot so that the feet are on line. Perform one round of covering and uncovering middle *dantian* with the cudgel in the right hand.

6) Hold the cudgel in the left hand. The right foot takes a step forward to form a bow step. Repeat the above movements in the opposite direction for four rounds with the left foot in front.

7) The left foot takes a step forward so that both feet are on line. Perform three rounds of covering and uncovering *dantian* to recover energy, then hold the cudgel in the right hand.

8) Tap lightly the inner *laogong* point (palm) of the left hand with the left end of the cudgel four times. As this is being done the left hand is in front of middle *dantian* and remains there motionless.

9) Following this, perform one round of covering and uncovering middle *dantian*. Then hold the cudgel in the left hand.

10) Tap *laogong* of the right hand with the right end of the cudgel four times.

11) Hold the cudgel with the right hand and perform three rounds of covering and uncovering middle *dantian*.

12) Place the *laogong* of the left hand on middle *dantian* and the right cudgel-holding hand on the left outer *laogong* (women reverse right and left). Perform three cycles of breathing. Drop the hands and stand relaxed and calm. After the mind is diverted from middle *dantian*, open the eyes slowly.

Mental Training

At the initial stage, you may leave out mental exercises, as it is enough to recall the forms and movements. But when you have a good command of the movements, your mind is easily distracted. That's why you have to set time for mental exercise appropriate to the level of your mastery of the other exercises.

Mental training means the concentration of such mental activities as consciousness, thinking and emotion during exercises on one point, one word or one subject so as to free yourself from various distracting thoughts. That is "to replace ten thousand ideas with one idea." In this way your cerebral cortex will gradually enter into a state in which the brain is neither excited, nor inhibited. You should do the exercise in a state of consciousness and should never be drowsy. Only when you are wide awake while doing the exercises can the cerebral cortex enjoy complete rest and regulation bringing about the desired therapeutic effect. Only in this way can all the organs and systems of the whole body be well protected and the vicious cycles of pathological inertia be stopped or suspended, paving the way for the body to create new cells.

The crux of the "New *Qigong* Therapy" lies in relaxation, tranquillity and concentration. Only when you keep your mind in perfect tranquillity, can you attain complete relaxation. Conversely, only when you maintain complete relaxation, can you keep your mind in perfect tranquillity. Only then can the inner vitality be brought about in great volume and smoothly circulated. Therefore mental training is the crux of the "New *Qigong* Therapy". You should practice hard and master it. The steps are as follows:

1. MIND FOCUSING

After getting familiar with the movements, novices should try to stop thinking about the movements when they practice.

Instead, they should think of a simple and unchanging word or phrase (like "health" or "overcome disease by exercising well"). Focus your mind on this subject matter.

2. SUBJECT SELECTION

After some time when you are more skilled at the forms and have basically mastered the exercise of mind focusing, you should move a step forward in your mental activities. That calls for subject selection.

To select a subject is to decide what to think about during your exercises, to think of one thing only and to get rid of various distracting thoughts so that the muscles, joints and brain can relax. This helps to give rise to inner vitality and is more therapeutic. You should get yourself ready for subject selection one day before your exercise so as to ensure that you select a subject most appropriate to your case and learn it by heart. But how do you select an appropriate subject?

1) First, think dialectically. You have to keep in mind the nature of your disease. For instance, patients of hypertension and high intraocular pressure caused by glaucoma should select something at a height lower than *qihai* point (such as flowers and grass on the ground, lawn, bushes etc.); while patients of hypotension and ptosis of inner organs should select something at a level higher than *yintang* point (such as tree-tops). Patients of normal blood pressure may select things on level with *shanzhong* point.

Moreover you have to take into consideration the location of your ailment. For instance, patients with liver trouble should avoid somberness and disturbances of mind. They ought to select something moderate and mild such as green trees or grass. Patients of heart trouble should avoid dazzling colors such as crimson. They may select purple or light red objects such as a red apple.

2) Select a simple and stable subject: Whatever you are going to select should help stabilize or focus your consciousness, thoughts and emotion and help you fall into a state of tranquil-

lity. Therefore the following points should be kept in mind: Select things around you rather than far from you. As beginners are less skillful they should pay attention to the distance of the object chosen. It should not be too far away. It would not be appropriate for someone to imagine himself touring the moon or recall a tree in his native town. Generally speaking, if you are practicing in a park, it would be better for you to choose something in the park to focus your attention on. Select still objects rather than things in motion: The object you choose should help to stabilize your consciousness, thoughts and emotions when you focus your mind on it. Therefore you should avoid anything which might excite you, such as willows swaying in the breeze, surging waves, fish swimming in water, elegant dancing, ball games or chess games. These are not appropriate subjects to choose. A placid lake or upright pine trees would be better subjects. You should avoid choosing scenes or things which might arouse emotional disturbance (such as poems or songs).

3) Select things beyond you, not things on your body, particularly at the initial stage. Do not change what you have chosen for your exercise. Stick to it for about three to six days until it cannot help you concentrate any more.

So far, we have touched upon methods of selecting a subject. Proper selection lays a solid foundation for holding on to the subject and attaining high therapeutic effect. Wrong selection may reduce the effect or even worsen your condition. This is something to be well noted.

3. SUBJECT HOLDING

This means that during exercises you think about the thing you have chosen, concentrating your mind on it. At any stage of mental exercise (mind focusing, subject selection, subject holding and mind concentration on *dantian*) you must act in line with the formula: "focus and diversion, spacious concentration, and hazy notion."

Focus and diversion

In doing exercises, no distracting thoughts are called for. If distracting thoughts happen to emerge you have to get rid of them by concentrating your mind on a certain subject. This is called focusing. Once the distracting thoughts are gone you may slacken your thought and put aside the subject for a little while. This is called diversion. At this time, you will have a more relaxed mind and loose form.

Spacious concentration

When focusing your mind on something, you should allow it to hover without overstraining; when diverting your mind, you should not keep it blank. Your mind is maintained in this state: neither concentrated nor diverged from the subject. Only in this way, can you stay relaxed and tranquil. This is called spacious concentration.

Hazy notion

When doing exercises, your mind should be in such a state that you seem to think of something and, at the same time, of nothing. Once you relax your mind, the subject disappears; if you draw back your attention, it returns. The subject seems to exist at a time and disappear at other times. Thus your mind will be naturally in a tranquil state.

To attain the above purposes, three principles must be observed: no forcing, no searching and no staring.

No forcing

When doing exercises, hold onto the subject, if you can. If not, do not try to force it to stay. Otherwise, dizziness and headache will develop.

No searching

When you cannot hold onto a subject, you may let it go for a while. Relax your mind a bit when distracting thoughts present themselves. Then the subject will come into your mind of its own. Do not try to search for it. Otherwise you will have such ailments as giddiness or palpitation.

No staring

When holding onto a subject you have to concentrate your mind on it. But it does not mean that you have to look at the image. The eyeballs should be kept in a position as if you were looking straight forward with the eyes closed. Actually there is nothing in front of you. For instance, if you choose an apple as the subject matter, the apple lingers in your mind. But you cannot put an apple actually in front of you. Consequently you have an apple in your mind, but you are not looking at an apple. If your sight falls upon an actual apple you will stare at it without turning your sight away. It will bring about less vital energy and can cause negative side effects.

How do you hold on to a subject well? This is the question any beginner will face. To hold on to a subject well demands coordination between regulation of postures and regulation of mind. During the preparatory exercises, think of *dantian* from the very beginning when you start relaxed standing, up to the exercise of three cycles of breathing. Then during the exercise of lifting-lowering-opening-closing, start to think of the subject when you lift the hands to *yintang*. The subject matter may leave you when you open up your hands, but it will come back naturally when you close up your hands. When you are lowering your hands, you have to keep the subject in your mind. You should never give way to impatience when distracting thoughts fall upon you and you fail to get rid of them. Try to remove them gradually. If you still fail to do so, you may relax your mind and body by standing firmly and performing three rounds of "lifting-lowering-opening-closing" without squatting down. The subject will come back naturally and you may continue with the exercises. At this stage, the subject seems almost nonexistant. Without persistant training you won't be able to scale this height. Neither will you be able to achieve that result by forcing or overdoing it. In addition, in coordination with this exercise you should also make strenuous efforts to practice the exercises of head massage and "rolling cudgel." Only then will you achieve relaxation, tranquillity, and natural posture, and promote a curative effect.

In case a beginner finds himself disturbed by the "seven human emotions," simply cannot get rid of distracting thoughts, and feels frustrated, he should by no means practice the exercises of falling into tranquillity (such as the slow pacing exercise, massage head and *yongquan* point). Otherwise, negative side effects could occur. In the above situation, you may stop to practice nasal respiration coordinated with fixed foot position or the exercise of respiration regulation or pacing exercise with moderate strength coordinated with nasal respiration. If you are startled while doing exercises you may stop to regulate your mind by doing three rounds of lifting-lowering-opening-closing and then continue doing the regular exercises.

If you are disturbed by outside noises (chirps of birds and cicadas, music, etc.), and you are unable to hold on to the subject, you may forget about it for a while and you may concentrate your mind on the disturbing noise instead. (The previously mentioned principles are still applicable.) When the disturbances are over, turn your mind back to the original subject. This is termed "occasional opening up" in mental training. (If the thing you choose to concentrate your attention on is at a level higher than "yintang" point it is called lifting method; if lower than *qihai* point, it is called lowering method; if it is as high as *shanzhong* point it is called deliberate opening method.)

4. ABANDONMENT OF SUBJECT

This means that when you do the concluding exercise you drop the subject which you have been holding on to by performing three rounds of lifting-lowering-opening-closing without squatting down. Direct your attention away from the subject you have chosen to middle *dantian*. When you are "playing with the ball," guide your mind back on to middle *dantian*. While the hands are playing the ball, the mind should be fixed on middle *dantian*, and not on the ball. When you release the ball, you abandon the subject completely. Nevertheless you should not allow your mind to drift along with the ball. Otherwise the vital energy will be impaired.

When you are kneading the abdomen your mind should be well-fixed on middle *dantian*. The mind should not follow the movements of the hands. After the kneading, do three cycles of breathing. Then raise both hands to perform the energy recovery exercise until the end of the concluding exercise. During the whole process of concluding exercise, fix your mind on *dantian*. Then stand motionless for a short while. Open your eyes slowly after your mind slowly leaves *dantian*. (This concluding exercise is called "closing up" of mental activity.)

These exercises can speed up the circulation of the blood and energy and increase internal secretions. At the initial stage of treatment through exercise, the chief purpose is to "turn saliva into essence of life."* Therefore, when saliva increases in the mouth after you are relaxed and calm, you should swallow it gulp by gulp down to middle *dantian* (*qihai*), passing through the throat and gastric cavity, where the saliva is gasified into essence. Moreover, after the exercises you must guide your vital energy in the body's various channels into *dantian* (*qihai*) through abandonment of the subject of concentration and transition of mind to *dantian*. After gasification, the vital energy is stored in the perineum. This is called "restoration of vital energy in the body." Persistent training will bring about vitality, improve physique and strengthen the body's immunization, thus building up the health and eliminating ailments. Therefore, select an appro-

---

*In traditional Chinese medicine, this refers to the fundamental substance which maintains the functioning of the body.

priate subject which is easy to hold onto and also easy to give up before you practice, and set aside enough time for the concluding exercise. The break-down of the timing is usually ten minutes for preparatory exercises, thirty to forty-five minutes for main exercises and ten to fifteen minutes for the concluding exercise, totaling one hour.

Basic Exercises for the Prevention and Treatment of Cancer

It is a theory of Chinese medicine that cancer is caused by imbalance of body fluids *(yin)* and vital energy *(yang)* and by stagnation of vital energy flow and the blood. "*Qigong*" therapy can have the effect of promoting the circulation of energy and blood, of building up health and relieving ailments, of abating swellings and undoing nodes and blockages. Therefore it is conducive to the treatment of cancer to persist in practicing "*Qigong*" exercises. Practical experience in China over the past ten years has shown that "*Qigong*" exercise can definitely prolong the life of cancer patients and alleviate their symptoms.

Some of the requirements and essentials of these exercises are similar to those of the élementary exercises. However elementary exercises are suited for ordinary chronic diseases, while these exercises are particularly suited for the prevention and treatment of cancer. (See Publisher's Note.)

1. PREPARATORY EXERCISE (SIMPLIFIED FORM)

Starting position:

Hold *dantian* with both hands.

Note:

The method is the same as that of the preparatory exercises in the beginning of this section on "New *Qigong*." The only difference here lies in the fact that cancer patients should first inhale steadily through the nose and then exhale steadily through the mouth three times each.

Method:

1) Perform three rounds of covering and uncovering middle *dantian*. Then you may start with the main exercise.

Note:

Hereafter, "steady respiration" refers to this sequence of movements.

2. PACING EXERCISES

The pacing exercise recommended below uses moderate strength in coordination with nasal respiration, and consists of six forms (A–F below):

A. Natural pacing with moderate strength in coordination with nasal respiration.

B. Pacing in place with moderate strength in coordination with respiration.

C. Stepping one pace with moderate strength in coordination with nasal respiration.

D. Stepping two paces with moderate strength in coordination with nasal respiration.

E. Stepping three paces with moderate strength in coordination with nasal respiration.

F. Fast pacing exercise with moderate strength in coordination with nasal respiration.

Note:

Pacing exercises are the most essential and effective forms of exercise in the "New *Qigong* Therapy" for the prevention and treatment of cancer and other difficult and complicated diseases.

The main points of pacing exercise are basically the same as those mentioned in the "Essentials for Exercises" in the first section of "New *Qigong* Therapy." What deserves our special emphasis again is regulation of mind. Try, as best you can, to remain calm and concentrated, relaxed and natural. In this way more vital energy will be produced and better results can be obtained.

In order to help you master the required skills of mental training, the main points are repeated as follows:

1. At the initial stage, you are only required to keep relaxed, calm and natural, to get familiar with the movements without paying too much attention to mental activities.

2. After a certain period of training after you have initially mastered the movements and respiration, you may choose a simple mental exercise to coordinate with the movements.

3. After a further period of training when you have basically reached a certain level of mastery, you may introduce the practice of mental training in accordance with your specific condition.

4. In order to further improve your skills, you may, in view of the actual level of your skill, either practice the exercise of "subject selection" or concentrate your mind on points of your own body (such as middle *dantian*).

A. NATURAL PACING WITH MODERATE STRENGTH IN COORDINATION WITH NASAL RESPIRATION

Note:

This exercise is basically the same as the "nasal respiration coordinated with fixed foot position" of the elementary exercises. The major difference lies in the fact that in doing the nasal respiration coordinated with fixed foot position you walk in a circle, while in this exercise you pace forward as if you were going for a stroll. To help you master this form, a brief introduction of its essentials is given below, in four sections:

Pacing exercise

Generally speaking, males move the left foot forward first and females move the right foot first. This is flexible and can vary according to different situations. For instance, hypertension and heart trouble patients of either sex can first move the left foot forward while patients with liver trouble can move the right foot forward first.

After the warm-up exercise, you may open your eyes slightly and walk ahead as if you were taking a stroll, but with special demands for the footwork.

When the left foot takes a step forward, put the heel gently down first with toes cocked up. Shift weight onto the left leg. After the left foot is placed naturally flat on the ground, the right foot starts to take a step forward in the same manner. Continue to move forward step by step in this fashion. While walking forward, keep the waist, lower back and hips relaxed, look straight ahead, eliminate distracting thoughts and put the tip of the tongue against the hard palate. The head turns gently from side to side together with body movement.

Arm-swing exercise

Simultaneously with the landing of the left foot, the right arm swings to the front of middle *dantian* and the left arm swings backward naturally to the side. When the right foot takes a step, the left arm swings to the front of middle *dantian* and the right arm swings backward to the side. The arms swing in coordination with the forward steps.

Points to Remember:

Don't start to swing the arm until the heel is on the ground. The palm is right in front of middle *dantian* only when the sole is completely on the ground. Keep the hand a fist's distance away from middle *dantian*.

The movements should be rhythmic, unstrained, relaxed and gay. The principles of roundness, softness and extensiveness must be applied. The armpits should be kept exposed throughout the exercise so as to ensure smooth circulation of vital energy.

Respiration exercise

Nasal respiration is used during the natural pacing exercise. By nasal respiration, we mean breathing through the nose, inhaling first and then exhaling. There is a slight breezy noise during inhalation. The noise should not be too loud, but just loud enough to be heard by yourself.

Two inhalations plus one exhalation make one breath in the nasal respiration for the natural pacing exercise, that is to say, when you place one foot on the ground you inhale twice. The moment you place the other foot on the ground, you exhale once. The two inhalations last almost as long as the one exhalation.

When you practice this exercise, you may also adopt what is referred to as "non-respiration" (forgetting deliberate respiration in order to breathe naturally). You may achieve better results if you practice nasal respiration and non-respiration alternately.

Concluding exercise

Return to the posture of relaxed standing. Stand there with eyes closed for a while. Perform three rounds of covering and uncovering middle *dantian* and three cycles of breathing.

Then stand relaxed and calm again. Knock the teeth and swallow saliva. Saliva may increase when you are pacing forward. Do not spit it out, but accumulate it in your mouth, and swallow slowly in either three or nine gulps when you are doing the concluding exercise. Imagine the saliva passing through the throat and stomach, finally reaching middle *dantian*. Then open your eyes and look straight ahead for a moment.

Points to remember:

Experience and observe the movements meticulously. Practice them scrupulously.

Walk fifteen minutes according to pattern. Then practice three cycles of breathing and three rounds of covering and uncovering middle *dantian*. All this together is one round. Do three rounds. In between each round, take a break and walk naturally for five to ten minutes. Weaker practitioners may sit down for a while after each round.

B. PACING EXERCISE IN PLACE WITH MODERATE STRENGTH IN COORDINATION WITH NASAL RESPIRATION.

Method:

The movements of this exercise are basically the same as those of the "pacing exercise with fixed foot position" in the elementary exercises. What distinguishes it is the method of breathing. This exercise adopts nasal respiration with moderate strength.

Note:

The outstanding feature of this exercise is that you practice at a fixed place. That makes it easier for you to choose a quiet environment full of fresh air. Because its movements and method of breathing are fixed, this exercise, like all other pacing exercises, is easier to master and persist in.

C. STEPPING ONE PACE WITH MODERATE STRENGTH IN COORDINATION WITH NASAL RESPIRATION.

Note:

The movements and essentials of this exercise are basically the same as those of "breathing with fixed foot position". But with this exercise, you must inhale twice and exhale once with one stride. Therefore it is an exercise of greater intensity and "offensive" in nature rather than "defensive" and suits patients with stronger constitutions. Patients with delicate constitutions should not practice this exercise until they feel stronger, and should first practice the exercise of stepping two paces with moderate strength in coordination with nasal respiration.

Functions:

This exercise can restore the balance of body fluids and vital energy. It has a good effect on tracheitis, pulmonary emphysema and influenza. It is also an effective means to prevent and treat cancer.

There are two different ways of doing this exercise. The warm-up exercise remains the same as before.

One pace exercise synchronized with inhalation when landing heel and exhalation when landing sole.

The movements and essential are almost the same as those in the "breathing exercises with fixed foot position", except when you step one pace you have to complete two inhalations and one exhalation, that is, inhalation-inhalation-exhalation. You inhale twice as soon as the heel touches the ground (with toes up) and exhale the moment the sole is put on the ground.

After twenty minutes of practice, rest for a few minutes. This is considered as one round. You can practice two rounds every morning. Patients with delicate constitutions do less.

**Tiptoe pacing exercise synchronized with
inhalation when landing heel and
exhalation when landing sole.**

This is similar to the one pace exercise with the only difference that after you complete the inhalation-inhalation-exhalation during one pace, move the other foot a step forward somewhere near the inner ankle of the front foot with the toes placed on the ground. This is intended to provide a little pause, and is called "smoothing the breath." You may stop your nasal respiration and breath normally, so that the energy and blood may flow more smoothly. Inhalation-inhalation-exhalation-pause constitute an entire process of respiration regulation.

D. STEPPING TWO PACES WITH MODERATE STRENGTH IN COORDINATION WITH NASAL RESPIRATION.

Method:

The movements and essentials of this exercise are basically the same as those of the "breathing with fixed foot position" with the only difference that you inhale twice as soon as you land the heel on the ground in every other forward step which is followed by one step of the other foot with the toes placed on the ground near the inner ankle of the front foot. Simultaneously with the follow-up toe-step movement, exhale once. Thus you inhale twice with every other step forward and exhale once when you follow it up with one step by the other foot. This makes one process of respiration of inhalation-inhalation-exhalation-pause.

Note:

This exercise is of mild intensity, but it can still fill your lungs with sufficient air, and therefore it is of high therapeutic value.

E. STEPPING THREE PACES WITH MODERATE STRENGTH COORDINATED WITH NASAL RESPIRATION

Method:

The movements and essentials of this exercise are basically the same as those of the form of "breathing with fixed foot position", with the only difference that you take one inhalation just as you land the heel with the first step; then you take another inhalation as soon as you land the heel with the second step. Then you exhale the moment you just put down the heel on the ground with the third step. Finally you move your rear foot a step forward somewhere near the inner ankle of the front foot with toes placed on the ground. Pause to "smooth" your breath. Repeat again and again.

Function:

This exercise is "defensive" in nature rather than "offensive." It is effective in the prevention and treatment of cancer. Moreover, it has a therapeutic effect on hypotension, anemia, leukopenia, chronic hepatitis, diabetes, arrhythmia and other heart troubles.

Note:

This exercise is suited for patients with delicate constitutions. Patients with extremely delicate constitutions may practice this exercise with eyes closed.

F. QUICK PACING EXERCISE SYNCHRONIZED WITH NASAL RESPIRATION.

Note:

This exercise can be classified into three forms, and is suited for early or medium stage cancer patients with strong constitutions. Advanced stage cancer patients must practice other exercises to build up their strength before they can start with this exercise.

Function:

The breath control part of this exercise gets rid of stale air and takes in fresh air, and can help regulate the circulation of energy, make the body supple, build up muscles, improve the complexion, enrich the texture of the muscles, bring about smooth circulation of saliva and blood, strengthen the physique, improve joint movements and cure disease. Again, you will get quicker results by coordinating nasal respiration with the exercise.

Method:

The movements and essentials are more or less the same as those of other pacing exercises with slight differences in breathing method and footwork. The three forms are as follows:

Pacing exercise synchronized with nasal respiration with a little strength:

After warming up, move one foot a step forward. Take two brief inhalations the moment you put the heel down. Move the other foot a step forward. Exhale once briefly as soon as the heel touches the ground. Thus inhale twice while taking one pace and exhale once while taking another pace. Continue to walk forward in this manner. Do not breathe with too much strength. Alternate the foot with which you start.

Pacing exercise synchronized with nasal respiration with moderate strength:

After warming up, move one foot a step forward. Inhale twice when the heel touches the ground. Exhale the moment you put down the sole, that is, inhale twice and exhale once while taking one pace. The movements are the same as other pacing exercises, but are faster than number 1 above. As this exercise needs greater intensity, you may speed up a bit.

**Pacing exercise synchronized with nasal
respiration with great strength:**

After warming up, move one foot a step forward. Inhale as soon as the heel touches the ground. At the same time, look straight ahead. Do not lower your head. Keep neck and hips relaxed, shoulders lowered. Thus you inhale while taking one pace and exhale while taking the next and so on. Alternate the foot with which you start. The two feet take turns to move forward first.

Note:

You may increase the intensity and speed of this exercise, but do not practice with undue haste. After every five or seven or nine steps you may stop to take a little rest to calm down. Then move the other foot forward first. Repeat these movements and then conclude as usual.

COURSE FOR TREATMENT OF CANCER

FIRST COURSE OF TREATMENT

This course lasts three months. Before starting, it is of paramount importance that you should first be confident in your struggle with cancer, shifting from a pessimistic attitude to an optimistic attitude. Secondly, choose the appropriate form of exercise in accordance with your condition and constitution.

Generally speaking, in the first month you practice the exercise of lifting-lowering-opening-closing and relaxed standing so as to ease the mind and body tension. Then you may take to nasal respiration with fixed foot position and the quick pacing exercise synchronized with nasal respiration with great strength (exhaling once while taking one pace and inhaling once while taking another pace). It is better to practice every morning in an environment full of fresh air. You should prolong the duration of the exercises and increase the number of repetitions gradually. But you should practice at least one and a half hours every day.

After one month's practice, add *"Qigong"* head massage to stimulate the body's nervous system to fight forcefully against the cancer.

In addition, you may also massage some of the acupuncture points along the channels pertinent to your disease. It must be noted that you can only massage the pressure points around the location of the malignancy so as to encircle and eliminate it. Never massage the malignancy itself or the place where the substance is located so as to avoid metastasis or proliferation of the carcinoma. For example, to strengthen the kidneys, nourish the liver and reinforce the heart, massage *yongquan*, and prevent the spread of carcinogenic substances into the liver through the kidneys. Patients with stomach cancer may massage stomach channels so as to protect the lungs and heart and strengthen the intestines and stomach, preventing the cancer from proliferating. Then when conditions permit, you may concentrate your efforts to eliminate the malignant substance itself. This is described as "encirclement without attack," cutting off the route of infiltration and eliminating the source of disease.

All in all, the first course of treatment is aimed at soothing the patient to create conditions for further treatment.

SECOND COURSE OF TREATMENT

This also lasts three months. Every day before sunrise, practice, for one hour, quick pacing exercise synchronized with nasal respiration with moderate strength where there is plenty of fresh air. (Practice twice. Half an hour for each time.)

When practicing this exercise, you draw in oxygen at each step. This exercise is most effective in building up health and destroying bacteria. But it is of minor intensity and moderate in nature. As a result the patient may practice with an easy mind.

Usually, during the second course of treatment, the symptoms are greatly reduced, confidence is increased and the health is built up. At this stage, slow pacing exercises synchronized with nasal respiration with moderate strength and regulation of sound production may be practiced to help the patient enter into a state of tranquillity and bring forth the vital energy needed to eliminate illness.

THIRD COURSE OF TREATMENT

After six months of training, you will experience a great change mentally. Your illness will have clearly taken a favorable turn. At this stage, in addition to quick pacing exercise synchronized with nasal respiration with moderate strength, you may add three inhalations and two exhalations or two inhalations and three exhalations in coordination with pacing exercises synchronized with nasal respiration and light massage on points. Usually this exercise is added only after nine months of training. Various forms of exercises may be practiced in coordination with this or practiced alternately with the aim of promoting and supplementing each other. These forms include slow pacing exercise synchronized with nasal respiration, various forms of *Qigong* massage, and regulation of sound production.

Points for attention:

The contents and duration of each course of treatment are flexible and vary according to the initiative of the practitioner, stage of treatment and change of conditions. Form and duration of exercises vary from patient to patient and from case to case. Nevertheless, each course of treatment must conform to the general objective.

The first course of treatment is aimed at easing the mind and curbing the ailment from worsening. This key phase may be called the stage of self-defense for which there are no short cuts. You must daily examine your exercise movements, postures, life-style and mood. Whenever you discover anything that hinders your regimen of exercise, you should get rid of it without delay. For instance, if a patient is disturbed by the "seven human emotions" (joy, anger, melancholy, brooding, sorrow, fear and shock), he must immediately suppress them. If there is a change in your condition, such as the occurrence of influenza, constipation and diarrhea, immediate treatment is called for. In winter, if the patient suffers from tracheitis, bronchitis or nasosinusitis, he should add the exercise of natural pacing synchronized with nasal respiration, laying emphasis on recuperation so that the main disease may be tackled later. Therefore, you should be flexible in choosing the forms of exercises and should not be rigid.

The second course of treatment is aimed at improving the patient's skill in exercise and his ability to resist disease so as to get ready for overall or partial attack on the focus of disease. This may be called a stage of stalemate.

The third course of treatment is aimed at eliminating virus and recovering health. As mentioned above, you may choose quite a number of forms of exercises in treating your disease. This phase may be termed the stage of overall counter-attack.

The above three courses have different objectives. As long as these objectives are reached, the forms and duration of practice are flexible and vary from person to person and from case to case.

V
Simplified
Taijiquan

Taijiquan is a precious part of China's national cultural heritage. Regular practice of *Taijiquan* can not only improve health and increase one's energy, but can prevent and cure certain diseases as well. It has been proven that *Taiji* can relieve greatly the effects of neurasthenia, ulcers, heart disease and tuberculosis.

Taijiquan is characterized by its soft, light, even, uninterrupted, smooth, natural, harmonious and coordinated movements. The exercises are especially suitable for older people and women.

The simplified *Taijiquan* included here is based on the traditional Chen School form and consists of twenty-four formal steps, or one hundred seventy-four movements. Of the various styles of *Taijiquan*, the Chen School is one of the most popular and has the longest history. The founder of the School was Chen Wangting who lived in Chenjiagon, Wen County, Henan Province during the late Ming and early Qing dynasties. The Chen School form was handed down from generation to generation. Chen Fake (1887–1957), a descendant of the original Chen family, was a noted contemporary exponent of the Chen School and author of a book entitled "Chen School *Taijiquan*" published in China.

Note:

Each exercise should go smoothly into the next one with no break in movement.

1. COMMENCING FORM

Method:

1) Stand naturally upright with the feet a shoulder-width apart, toes pointing straight forward, hands at sides, arms hanging naturally. Look straight ahead. (*Fig. 264*)

Points to remember:

Keep head and neck upright, with chin drawn slightly inward. Do not deliberately protrude chest or draw abdomen in. Relax and concentrate.

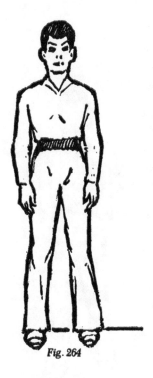

Fig. 264

2) Slowly raise the arms forward and upward to shoulder level with palms facing downward. *(Figs. 265–266)*

3) Keep the torso straight. Press the hands down gently, bending the knees. Look straight ahead. *(Fig. 267)*

Points to remember:

Hold the shoulders and elbows down. Keep the fingers slightly bent. Weight should be equally distributed on both legs. While bending the knees, keep the lower back relaxed and buttocks slightly pulled in. The lowering of the arms should be coordinated with the bending of the knees.

Fig. 265

Fig. 266

Fig. 267

2. PART THE WILD HORSE'S MANE TO LEFT AND RIGHT

Starting Position:

Continue from commencing form.

Method:

1) Turn the torso slightly to the right and shift weight onto right leg. Raise the right hand to the front of the right chest with palm facing downward, while the left hand moves up to waist level, palm facing upward, as if holding a ball with both hands. Move left foot closer to the right foot and pick up the left heel. Look at the right hand. *(Figs. 268–269)*

Fig. 268   Fig. 269

2) Turn the torso to the left and move left foot a step forward to the left. Bend the left knee and shift weight onto the left leg. Keep the right leg straight with heel pressing down on the floor to form a left bow stance. At the same time, gradually raise the left forearm obliquely to eye level, palm facing obliquely upward, elbow slightly bent with the right hand dropping to the side of right hip, palm facing downward, fingers pointing forward. Look at the left hand. (*Figs. 270–271*)

3) Lean back slowly and shift weight onto the right leg. Raise the toes of the left foot slightly off the ground and turn them outward. Then bend the left leg, turn the body to the left and shift weight back again onto the left leg. Return hands to a ball-holding position in front of the left part of the chest with

Fig. 270

Fig. 271

the left hand on top. Then draw the right foot, heel up, forward towards the left foot which is now flat on the ground. Look at the left hand. (*Fig. 272–273*)

4) Take a right bow step by moving the right foot a step forward, straightening the left leg with the heel pressing down on the floor, bending the right leg at knee. At the same time, turn the torso to the right, gradually raising the right hand obliquely upward to eye level with palm facing obliquely upward, elbow slightly bent and press the left hand down to the left hip with palm facing downward and fingers pointing forward. Look at the right hand. (*Figs. 274–275*)

5) Repeat No. 3 reversing right and left.

6) Repeat No. 4 reversing right and left.

Fig. 272

Fig. 273

Points to remember:

Hold the torso upright and keep the chest relaxed. Arms should move in an arc. Keep the arms from being fully stretched when separating the hands. In turning the body, the waist serves as the axis. Movements in taking bow step and in separating hands must be even and synchronized. When taking a bow step, place the foot slowly in position with the heel coming down first. The knee of the front leg should not go beyond the toes; the rear leg should straighten backward a bit. The rear foot should form an angle of forty-five to sixty degrees to the front foot. Heels should not be placed on a straight line and the transverse distance between them should be four to twelve inches.

3. WHITE CRANE SPREADS ITS WINGS

Starting Position:

Continue from preceding Exercise 2.

Fig. 274

Fig. 275

Method:

1) Turn the torso slightly to the left and form a ball-holding gesture in front of the left chest with the left hand on top. Look at the left hand. *(Fig. 276)*

2) Draw the right foot a step towards the left foot and then shift weight onto the right leg. Turn torso slightly to the right. Move the left foot slightly forward and rest its toes lightly on the floor. At the same time, turn the torso slightly to the left. Raise the right hand toward the right temple with palm facing left, at the same time moving the left hand downward to the left hip with palm facing downward and fingers pointing forward. Look straight ahead. *(Figs. 277)*

Points to remember:

Do not thrust chest forward. Arms should be rounded when they move up or down. Slightly bend the left leg at knee. Coordinate backward weight shift with the raising of the right hand.

Fig. 276

Fig. 277

4. BRUSH KNEE AND TWIST STEP ON BOTH SIDES

Starting Position:

Continue from preceding Exercise 3.

Method:

1) The right hand moves downward while the left hand moves upward. The right hand circles down past the abdomen and then backwards and upward to ear level with the arm slightly bent and palm facing obliquely upward. At the same time, the left hand moves first in an upward and then in a downward curve ending at the right part of the chest with palm facing obliquely downward. At the same time, turn the torso slightly to the left and then to the right. Look at the right hand. *(Figs. 278–280)*

2) Turn the torso to the left. The left foot takes one step forward to form a left bow step. At the same time, push forward with the right hand past the right ear at nose level with palm facing forward. The left hand drops and brushes past the left knee and stops beside the left hip with palm facing downward. Look at fingers of the right hand. *(Figs. 281–282)*

3) Sit back with right knee shifting weight onto the right leg, now bent. Raise the left toes and turn the left foot a bit outward. Then bend the left leg slowly. Turn body to the left and shift weight onto the left leg. Bring the right foot forward to the side of the left foot and rest its toes on floor. At the same time, turn the left palm upward with elbow slightly bent and move the left hand sideways and up to shoulder level with palm turning obliquely upward, while the right hand, following the turning of the torso, makes an arc upward and then downward to the left ending in front of the left part of the chest with palm facing obliquely downward. Look at the left hand. *(Figs. 283–284)*

Fig. 278

Fig. 279

Fig. 280

Fig. 281

Fig. 282

4) Repeat No. 2, reversing right and left.
5) Repeat No. 3, reversing right and left.
6) Repeat No. 2.

Points to remember:

Keep the torso upright, shoulders and elbows down while pushing hands forward. Waist, lower back and hips should be relaxed. Movements of the palm should be coordinated with those of the waist and legs. In taking a bow step, transverse distance between the heels should not be less than twelve inches.

5. STRUM THE LUTE

Starting Position:

Continue from preceding Exercise 4.

Method:

1) Move the right foot half a step forward towards the left heel. Sit back and turn torso slightly to the right, shifting weight onto the left leg. Raise the left foot and place it slightly forward with the heel on the floor and the knee bent a little.
2) At the same time, raise the left hand forward in a curve to nose level with the palm facing the right and the elbow slightly bent, drawing the right hand downward to the inside of the left elbow, palm facing left. Look at the forefinger of the left hand. *(Figs. 285–287)*

Points to remember:

Body position should remain steady and natural with chest relaxed and shoulders and elbows held down. The left hand should be raised more or less in a circular movement. In moving the right foot half a step forward, place it slowly in position with toes coming down first. Weight transfer must be coordinated with the movement of the hands.

Fig. 283

Fig. 284

Fig. 285

Fig. 286

Fig. 287

6. STEP BACK AND WHIRL ARMS ON BOTH SIDES

Starting Position:

Continue from preceding Exercise 5.

Method:

1) Turn the torso slightly to the right. The right hand makes a semicircle past the abdomen and proceeds backward and upward to shoulder level with palm facing upward and arm slightly bent. Turn the left palm up and place the toes of the left foot on the floor (heel up). First look to the right as body turns in that direction, then turn to look at the left hand. (*Figs. 288–289*)

2) Bend right arm and draw the right hand past the right ear before pushing it ahead with palm facing forward. Pull the left hand back to the waist with palm facing upward. At the same time, raise the left foot lightly and take a step backward,

Fig. 288   Fig. 289

placing the foot slowly down toes first, then heel. Keep weight on the left leg and form a right empty step. Eyes look first to the left as the body turns in that direction, then turn to look at the right hand. *(Figs. 290–291)*

3) Repeat No. 2, reversing right and left.
4) Repeat No. 2.
5) Repeat No. 2, reversing right and left.

Points to remember:

In pushing out or drawing back, the hands should move in an arc. While pushing out the hands, keep the lower back, waist and hips relaxed. The speed of the hand movements should be the same. When stepping back, place the toes down first and then slowly set the whole foot on the floor. While turning the body, turn the front foot until it comes in line with the body, pivoting on the toes. When taking a step backward, move one leg slightly towards the other, taking care not to let the feet land in a straight line. Then turn to look at the hand in front.

Fig. 290

Fig. 291

7. GRASP THE BIRD'S TAIL TO THE LEFT

Starting Position:

Continue from preceding Exercise 6.

Method:

1) Turn the torso slightly to the right. Drop the left hand past the abdomen, palm facing upward and bend the right elbow to form a ball-holding gesture in front of the right part of the chest with the right hand on top. At the same time, shift weight onto the right leg, drawing the left foot to the side of the right foot and rest its toes on the floor. Look at the right hand. (*Figs. 292–293*)

2) The left foot takes a step forward to the left, turning the torso slightly to the left. Bend the left leg to form a left bow step with the right leg naturally straightened. Meanwhile, push out the rounded left forearm at shoulder level with palm facing inward. The right hand drops at the same time slowly

Fig. 292

Fig. 293

to the right hip, palm facing downward, finger pointing forward. Look at the left forearm. *(Figs. 294–295)*

Points to remember:

Keep both arms rounded, while pushing out. The separation of the hands, relaxation of the waist and bending of the leg must be coordinated.

3) Turn the torso slightly to the left. Simultaneously, extend the left hand forward with palm facing downward. Bring the right hand upward with palm facing upward, until it is below the left forearm. Then turn the torso to the right, while pulling both hands down in such a way as to draw an arc before the abdomen, with the right hand extending sideways at shoulder level, palm facing upward, and left forearm across the chest with palm facing inward. While doing this, shift weight onto the right leg. Look at the right hand. *(Figs. 296–298)*

Fig. 294

Fig. 295

Fig. 296

Fig. 297

Fig. 298

Points to remember:

While lowering the hands, do not lean forward or let the buttocks protrude. The arms should follow the turning of the waist and move in an arc.

4) Turn the torso slightly to the left. Bend the right arm and place the right hand inside the left wrist. Turn the torso a little further to the left. Press both hands slowly forward with the right palm facing forward and the left palm inward. The left arm must be rounded. Meanwhile, shift weight slowly onto the left leg to form a bow step. Look at the left wrist. *(Figs. 299–300)*

Points to remember:

Keep the torso upright when pressing the hands forward. The movement of the hands must be coordinated with the relaxing of the waist and the bending of the leg.

Fig. 299

Fig. 300

Fig. 301

Fig. 302

5) Turn both palms downward as the right hand passes over the left wrist, moving forward and to the right to keep it at the same level with the left hand. Separate the hands a shoulder-width apart and sit back, shifting weight onto the slightly bent right leg, with toes of the left foot up (heel down). Draw back both hands to the front of the abdomen, palms facing slightly downward to the front. Look straight ahead. *(Figs. 301–302)*
6) Slowly transfer weight onto the left leg, while pushing hands forward and obliquely upward with palms facing forward at shoulder level. At the same time, bend the left knee to form a left bow step. Look straight ahead. *(Figs. 303–304)*

Points to remember:

In pushing hands forward, the hands should move in a curve with wrists at shoulder level and elbows slightly bent.

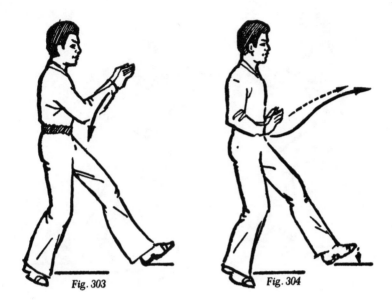

Fig. 303   Fig. 304

8. GRASP THE BIRD'S TAIL TO THE RIGHT

Starting Position:

Continue from preceding Exercise 7.

Method:

1) Sit back and turn the torso to the right, shifting weight onto the right leg and turn the toes of the left foot inward. The right hand makes an arc to the right, then moves downward past the abdomen and upward towards the left ribs, palm upward, and forms a ball-holding gesture with the left hand on top. Meanwhile, weight is shifted back onto the left leg. Place the right foot beside the left foot with heel raised. Look at the left hand. *(Figs. 305–308)*

2) Repeat No. 2 of Exercise 7, reversing right and left.

3) Repeat No. 3 of Exercise 7, reversing right and left.

4) Repeat No. 4 of Exercise 7, reversing right and left.

Fig. 305

Fig. 306

5) Repeat No. 5 of Exercise 7, reversing right and left.
6) Repeat No. 6 of Exercise 7, reversing right and left.

Points to remember:

The same as in Exercise 7.

9. SINGLE WHIP

Starting Position:

Continue from preceding exercise 8.

Method:

1) Sit back and gradually shift weight onto the left leg, turning the toes of the right foot inward. Meanwhile, turn the body to the left and move both hands leftward with left hand on top, until the left arm is extended sideways at shoulder level with palm facing outward, and the right hand is in front of left lower ribs with palm facing obliquely inward. Look at the left hand. *(Figs. 313–314)*

Fig. 307

Fig. 308

Fig. 313

Fig. 314

2) Turn the body to the right and shift weight gradually onto the right leg. Draw the left foot to the inside of the right foot with the toes of the left foot touching the floor. At the same time, the right hand makes an upward and rightward curve with the arm at shoulder level. With the right palm now turned somewhat outward, bunch the fingertips together and turn them downward at the wrist to form a "hooked hand," while the left hand simultaneously moves in an arc past the abdomen and stops in front of the right shoulder, palm facing inward. Look at the left hand. (*Figs. 315–316*)

Fig. 315

Fig. 316

3) Turn the body to the left, taking a step forward with the left foot. Bend the left knee into a bow stance. While shifting weight onto the left leg, rotate the left palm slowly and push it ahead facing front with fingertips at eye level and elbow slightly bent. Look at the left hand. *(Figs. 309–310)*

Points to remember:

Keep the torso upright and waist and lower back relaxed. The right elbow should be slightly bent downward the left elbow directly above the left knee. Keep the shoulders down. The left palm turns as it presses forward. Do not turn it too quickly or abruptly. All transitional movements must be well coordinated.

Fig. 309

Fig. 310

Fig. 311

Fig. 312

10. WAVE HANDS LIKE CLOUDS TO THE LEFT

Starting Position:

Continue from preceding Exercise 9.

Method:

1) Shift weight onto the right leg and turn the body gradually to the right, turning the toes of the left foot inward. The left hand makes an arc past the abdomen and stops in front of the right shoulder, palm obliquely inward. At the same time, unhook the right hand and turn the palm outward. Look at the left hand. *(Figs. 311–312)*

2) Turn the torso gradually to the left and shift weight onto the left leg. The left hand makes an arc past the face with the palm turning slowly outward. The right hand makes an arc past the abdomen and then upward to the left shoulder with palm turned obliquely inward. At the same time, bring the right foot to the side of the left foot so that feet are parallel, four to eight inches apart. Look at the right hand. *(Figs. 317–319)*

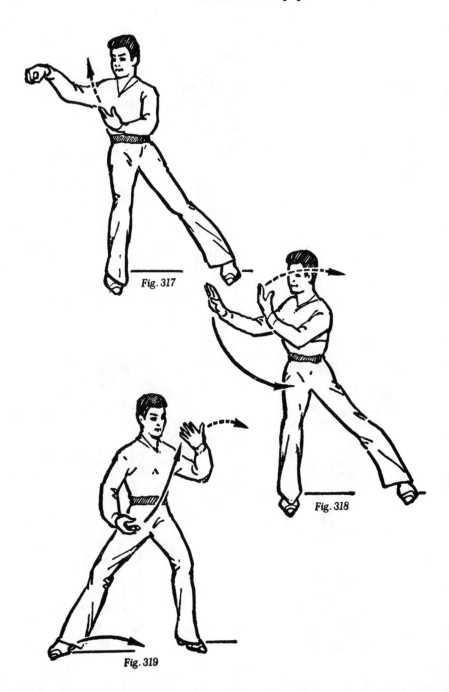

Fig. 317

Fig. 318

Fig. 319

Fig. 320

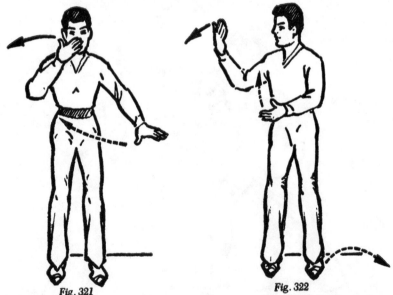

Fig. 321

Fig. 322

3) Turn the torso gradually to the right and shift weight onto the right leg. The right hand continues to move to the right side past the face, where the palm turns outward, while the left hand makes an arc past the abdomen and upward to shoulder level with palm turned obliquely inward. The left foot takes a side step at the same time. Look at the left hand. *(Figs. 320–322)*

4) Repeat No. 2.
5) Repeat No. 3.
6) Repeat No. 2.

Points to remember:

The lumbar vertabrae serve as the axis for the torso's turns. Keep the waist, lower back and hips relaxed and avoid a sudden rise or fall of body position. Movement of the arms should be natural and circular and should follow the movements of the waist. The pace must be slow and even. Maintain balance when moving lower limbs. The eyes should follow the hand when it moves past the face.

11. SINGLE WHIP

Starting Position:

Continue from preceding Exercise 10.

Method:

1) Turn the torso to the right. At the same time, the right hand moves towards the right side and forms a hooked hand at a point a little higher than shoulder level, while the left hand makes an arc past the abdomen and then upward to the right shoulder with palm turned inward. While moving the arms, shift weight onto the right leg and lift the left heel off the ground. Look at the left hand. *(Figs. 323–325)*
2) Repeat No. 3 of Exercise 9. *(Figs. 326–327)*

Points to remember:

The same as in Exercise 9.

Fig. 323

Fig. 324

Fig. 325

Fig. 326   Fig. 327

12. HIGH PAT ON HORSE

Starting Position:

Continue from preceding Exercise 11.

Method:

1) The right foot takes half a step forward. Shift weight onto the right leg. Unhook the right hand and turn both palms upward with the elbows slightly bent, while the body turns slightly to the right, the left heel gradually coming off the ground to form an empty step. Look at the left hand. (*Fig. 328*)

2) Turn the torso slightly to the left and draw the right hand past the right ear, pushing it forward with palm facing front and fingers pointing up at eye level. Lower the left hand to the front of the left hip with palm still facing upward. At the same time, bring the left foot slightly forward with heel up. Look at the right hand. (*Fig. 329*)

Fig. 328

Fig. 329

Points to remember:

Hold the torso upright and relaxed. Keep the shoulders low and bend the right elbow slightly downward.

13. KICK WITH RIGHT HEEL

Starting Position:

Continue from preceding Exercise 12.

Method:

1) Cross the hands by extending the left hand, palm upward, onto the back of the right wrist. Then separate the hands, each making an arc downward with palms turned obliquely downward. At the same time, the left foot is raised and takes a step forward, forming a left bow step, toes turned slightly outward. Look straight ahead. (*Figs. 330–332*)

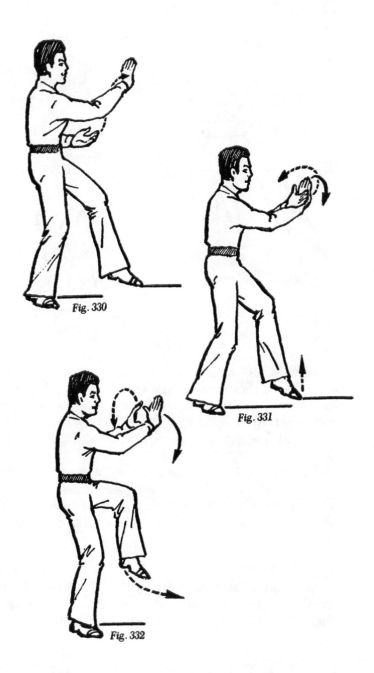

Fig. 330

Fig. 331

Fig. 332

Fig. 333

Fig. 334

2) Both hands continue to circle outward and then back around until they cross in front of chest, both palms turned inward, with the back of the left hand against the inside of the right wrist. At the same time, bring the right foot to the side of the left foot, toes resting on floor. Look to the right. (*Fig. 333*)

3) Separate the hands, extending them sideways at shoulder level, with elbows slightly bent and palms turned outward. At the same time, raise the right leg, bent at the knee, and thrust the foot gradually forward. Look at the right hand. (*Figs. 334–335*)

Points to remember:

Keep your balance. Keep the wrists at shoulder level when the right foot kicks forward. The force of the kick should be from the heel, with the upturned toes pointing, hooking

Fig. 335

Fig. 336

slightly backward. The separation of the hands should be coordinated with the kick. The right arm should be parallel with the right leg.

14. STRIKE OPPONENT'S EARS WITH BOTH FISTS

Starting Position:

Continue from preceding Exercise 13.

Method:

1) Draw back the right foot and raise the knee. At the same time, move the left hand upward and forward, then downward and parallel to the right hand in front of chest. Turn both palms up. Drop down hands in an arc to both sides of the right knee. Look straight ahead. *(Figs. 336–337)*

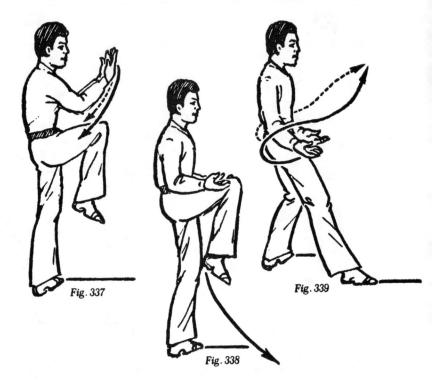

Fig. 337

Fig. 338

Fig. 339

2) The right foot lands slowly on the floor at a point slightly to the right and in front of the left foot. Shift weight onto the right leg to form a bow step. At the same time, drop both hands and gradually clench the fists which move upward and forward in an arc from the sides to the front of the head like a pincer, knuckles facing obliquely upward. The distance between fists is about four to eight inches. Look at the right fist. (*Figs. 338–339*)

Points to remember:

Hold the head and neck upright. Keep the waist and lower back relaxed and the fists loosely clenched. Keep the shoulders low and allow the elbows to fall naturally with arms slightly bent.

Fig. 340

Fig. 341

15. TURN AND KICK WITH LEFT HEEL

Starting Position:

Continue from preceding Exercise 14.

Method:

1) Bend the left leg and sit back. Turn the body to the left, pivoting the right foot on the heel so that the toes point inward. Simultaneously, open the fists and separate the hands in a circular movement and extend them sideways, left and right, a little above shoulder level, palms facing forward. Look at the left hand. *(Figs. 340–341)*

Fig. 342

Fig. 343

2) Shift weight onto the right leg. Bring the left foot to the inside of the right foot with toes on the floor. At the same time, circle both hands downward to the sides and then up, crossing wrists in front of the chest, with the back of the right hand against the inside of the left wrist, both palms facing inward. Look forward to the left. (*Figs. 342–343*)

3) Separate the hands and extend them sideways left and right at shoulder level, with elbows slightly bent and palms facing outward. At the same time, raise the left leg with knee bent and then thrust the foot gradually forward. Look at the left hand. (*Figs. 344–346*)

Points to remember:

The same as in Exercise 13, reversing right and left.

Fig. 344

Fig. 345

Fig. 346

16. SQUAT DOWN AND STAND ON ONE LEG—LEFT STYLE

Starting Position:

Continue from preceding Exercise 15.

Method:

1) Draw back the left foot, bent at the knee so that the thigh is parallel with the ground. Turn the torso to the right. At the same time, form a right hooked hand, while the left palm is turned up and makes an arc to the right side in front of the right shoulder and faces obliquely inward. Look at the right hand. *(Figs. 347–348)*

Fig. 347

Fig. 348

2) Stretch the left leg slightly backward and down to the side and crouch down slowly on the right leg. The left hand is extended sideways along the inner side of the left leg with palm facing forward. Look at the left hand. *(Figs. 349–350)*

Points to remember:

When the right leg is bent in a full crouch, turn the toes of the right foot slightly outward and straighten the left leg with the toes turned slightly inward; both soles are flat on the floor. Keep the toes of the left foot in line with the heel of the right foot. Do not lean the upper part of the body too far forward.

Fig. 349

Fig. 350

3) Using the heel as pivot, turn the toes of the left foot slightly outward and turn the toes of the right foot inward. Shift weight onto the left leg, forming a bow stance to the left. The torso turns slightly to the left and then rises slowly in a forward movement. At the same time, the left arm continues to extend forward, with palm facing right, while the right hand drops behind the back, bunched fingertips pointing backward. Look at the left hand. *(Fig. 351)*

4) Raise the right foot gradually and bend right knee so that thigh is parallel with the ground. At the same time, open the right hand and swing it past the right leg and upward to the front, until the bent elbow is just above the right knee, fingers pointing up and palm facing left. Lower the left hand to the left hip, palm facing downward. Look at the right hand. *(Figs. 352–353)*

Fig. 351

Points to remember:

Keep the torso upright. Bend the standing leg slightly. The toes should point naturally downward as the right foot is raised.

17. SQUAT DOWN AND STAND ON ONE LEG TO THE RIGHT STYLE

Starting Position:

Continue from preceding Exercise 16.

Method:

1) Put the right foot down in front of the left foot, its toes resting on the floor. Turn body to the left, pivoting on the balls

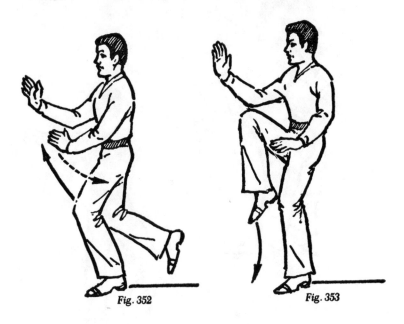

Fig. 352   Fig. 353

of the left foot. At the same time, the left hand is raised sideways and upward to shoulder level and turns into a hooked hand, while the right hand, following the torso, moves in a backward arc around to the front of the left shoulder, fingers pointing up. Look at the left hand. (*Figs. 354–355*)

2) Repeat No. 2 of Exercise 16, reversing right and left.
3) Repeat No. 3 of Exercise 16, reversing right and left.
4) Repeat No. 4 of Exercise 16, reversing right and left.

Points to remember:

Raise the right foot slightly before crouching over the left leg and stretching the right leg sideways. Everything else is the same as in Exercise 16, except that right and left are reversed.

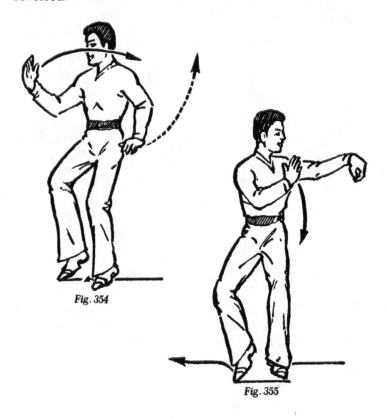

Fig. 354

Fig. 355

18. PASS THE SHUTTLE LEFT AND RIGHT

Starting Position:

Continue from preceding Exercise 17.

Method:

1) Turn the body to the left. The left foot lands on the floor in front of the right foot, with toes pointing outward. With the right heel slightly raised, bend both knees to form a semi-cross-legged posture. At the same time, form a ball-holding gesture before the left chest with the left hand on top. Then move right foot over to the left foot, toes resting on floor. Look at the left forearm. (*Figs. 356–358*)

Fig. 356

Fig. 357

Fig. 358

Fig. 359

Fig. 360

Fig. 361

2) The body turns to the right and the right foot takes a step forward to form a bow step. At the same time, the right hand moves upward, stopping just above the right temple, palm turned obliquely upward. The left hand first moves downward to the left side and then pushes forward at nose level, palm facing forward. Look at the left hand. *(Figs. 359–361)*

3) Turn the body slightly to the right, shifting weight slightly backward, with the toes of right foot turned outward a bit. Then shift weight back onto the right leg. Place the left foot alongside the right foot, toes resting on the floor. At the same time, make a ball-holding gesture in front of the right chest, right hand on top. Look at the right forearm. *(Figs. 362–363)*

4) Repeat No. 2, reversing right and left.

Points to remember:

Do not lean forward when pushing hands forward or shrug shoulders when raising hands. Movements of the hands should be coordinated with the waist and legs. The distance between the heels in the bow step should be about twelve inches.

Fig. 362

Fig. 363

19. NEEDLE AT THE BOTTOM OF THE SEA

Starting Position:

Continue from preceding Exercise 18.

Method:

1) The right foot takes half a step forward. Shift weight onto the right leg as the left foot moves forward a bit, toes resting on the floor to form a left empty step. At the same time, turn the body slightly to the right and lower the right hand in front of body, then raising it up and back to the right ear.

2) From there with the body slightly turning towards the left, thrust the right hand obliquely downward. Simultaneously, the left hand makes an arc forward and downward to the left hip, palm facing downward, fingers pointing forward. Look at the floor ahead. *(Figs. 364–365)*

Points to remember:

Turn the body first slightly to the right and then to the left. Do not lean too far forward. Keep the head up and buttocks in. The left leg should be slightly bent.

20. FLASH THE ARMS

Starting Position:

Continue from preceding Exercise 19.

Method:

1) Turn the body slightly to the right. The left foot takes a step forward to form a bow step. At the same time, raise the right arm with elbow bent until the hand stops just above the right temple.

2) Turn the palm obliquely upward with the thumb pointing downward. Raise the left hand slightly and push it forward at nose level with palm facing forward. Look at the left hand. *(Figs. 367–369)*

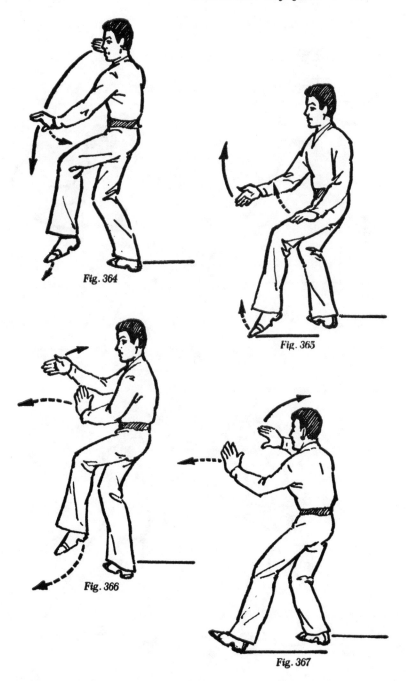

Fig. 364

Fig. 365

Fig. 366

Fig. 367

Fig. 368

Fig. 369

Fig. 370

Points to remember:

Hold the torso in an upright and natural position. Relax the waist and hips. Do not straighten the left arm. Keep the muscles of the back relaxed. The movement of the palm pushing forward should be coordinated with the taking of the bow step.

21. TURN TO STRIKE, PARRY AND PUNCH

Starting Position:

Continue from preceding Exercise 20.

Method:

1) Sit back and shift weight onto the right leg. The body turns to the right, with the toes of the left foot turned inward. Then shift weight again onto the left leg. As the torso turns, the right hand circles towards the right and downward and then, with fingers clenched into a fist, moves past abdomen to the

Fig. 371

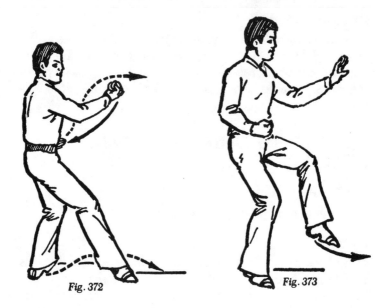

Fig. 372

Fig. 373

left side, back of the hand up. At the same time, raise the left arm above head with palm turned obliquely upward. Look straight ahead. *(Figs. 370–371)*

2) Turn the body to the right. The right fist thrusts upward and forward across the chest with knuckles turned down while the left hand drops to the left hip, palm turned downward and fingers pointing forward. At the same time, withdraw the right foot and immediately take a step forward, toes turned outward. Look at the right fist. *(Figs. 371–372)*

3) Shift weight onto the right leg and take one step forward with the left foot. At the same time, parry with the left hand moving up and forward from the left in an arc and pull the right fist in a curve back to the right waist, knuckles turned downward. Look at the left hand. *(Figs. 373–374)*

4) The left leg bends to form a bow step. At the same time, the right fist strikes forward at chest level with the back of hand facing right. Pull the left hand simultaneously back to the right inner forearm. Look at the right fist. *(Fig. 375)*

Fig. 374

Fig. 375

Points to remember:

Clench the right fist loosely. While pulling back the fist, the forearm is first turned inward and then outward. As the fist strikes forward, the right shoulder extends a bit forward. Hold the shoulders and elbows down. The right arm should be slightly bent.

22. DRAW BACK AND PUSH

Starting Position:

Continue from preceding Exercise 21.

Method:

1) The left hand stretches forward from below the right wrist as the right fist opens. Turn both palms up, separate hands and pull back slowly. At the same time, sit back with the toes

Fig. 376   Fig. 377

of the left foot off the ground, weight shifted onto the right leg. Look straight ahead. *(Figs. 376–377)*

2) Turn the palms down in front of the chest, then push downward past the abdomen and then forward and upward. Keep the wrists at shoulder level with palms facing forward. At the same time, shift weight onto the left leg to form a bow step. Look ahead. *(Figs. 378–380)*

Points to remember:

Do not lean backward when sitting back. Keep the buttocks in. Relax the shoulders and turn the elbows a bit outward as the bent arms are pulled back. Do not pull arms back straight. The extended hands should be separated at a distance not wider than the shoulders.

23. CROSS HANDS

Starting Position:

Continue from preceding Exercise 22.

Fig. 378

Fig. 379

Fig. 380

Fig. 381   Fig. 382

Method:

1) Bend the right knee and shift weight onto the right leg. Turn the torso to the right as the toes of the left foot lift and turn inward. Both hands swing in two arcs left and right at shoulder level, with palms facing forward and elbows slightly bent. At the same time, the right foot turns slightly outward and weight is shifted onto the right leg to form a side bow step. Look at the right hand. (*Figs. 381–383*)

2) Slowly shift weight onto the left leg, turning the right foot inward. Then the right foot moves towards the left foot so that the two feet are parallel and a shoulder-width apart. Gradually straighten the legs. At the same time, move both hands in downward arcs and then upward past the abdomen, crossing in front of the chest, palms facing inward, with wrists at shoulder level, right hand on the outside. Look straight ahead. (*Figs. 384–385*)

Points to remember:

Do not lean forward when separating or crossing the hands. When straightening the legs, keep the torso naturally erect

Fig. 383

Fig. 384

Fig. 385

with head held straight up, chin drawn slightly inward. Keep the arms rounded in a comfortable position with shoulders and elbows down.

24. CLOSING FORM

Starting Position:

Continue from preceding Exercise 23.

Method:

Turn the palms forward then downward and lower both hands gradually to the sides. Look straight ahead. (*Figs. 386–387*)

Points to remember:

Keep the whole body relaxed and slowly exhale as the hands are lowered. Bring the left foot alongside the right foot after the breath has returned to normal and walk about for a little while before resuming usual activities.

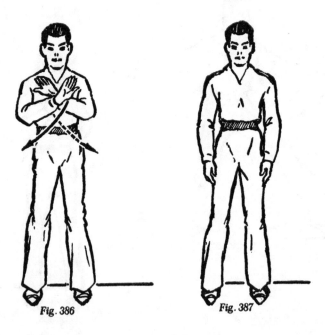

Fig. 386   *Fig. 387*

VI

Thirty Recipes for Medical Treatment and Health Care

The recipes included here can serve both as tasty, nutritious dishes, as well as medicinal tonics. Food and herbal medicine share similar origins. The Chinese people have attached great importance to the summing up of experience in this field since ancient times. As early as the Western Zhou Dynasty over three thousand years ago, there existed in China governmental offices in charge of "dietetic treatment." The sole responsibility of the officials of these offices was to prepare nourishing food for emperors and to ensure their health. Many books on diet-therapy or nutrition were written in later dynasties such as "Herbs for Diettherapy", and "Properties of Edible Herbs" in the Tang Dynasty (618–907 A.D.); "Herbs for Daily Use", "Guide to Dietetics" in the Yuan Dynasty (1271–1368 A.D.); and "Eatable Herbs", "Outline of Edible Herbs" and "Herbs Useful During Famine" in the Ming (1368–1644 A.D.) and Qing Dynasties (1644–1911). To date, over fifty of these books are known to the modern generation. The recipes in this book have been carefully selected from these treatises and from popular folk recipes. These recipes, traditionally used for the prevention and cure of common diseases of middle-aged and old people, are easy to prepare, and have been proven to be effective through the practice of the masses. In America, most of the ingredients are available in Chinatown markets and at herbal pharmacies.

As the saying goes, "An ounce of prevention is worth a pound of cure." It is our belief that by combining recipes appropriate to season and individual constitution with physical exercise, anyone can improve his health and live a longer, happier life.

Note:

The metric system is used here. Approximate equivalents in ounces are provided. If the reader wishes to compute conversions exactly, he should multiply the figure in grams by 0.035 to obtain the amount in ounces.

In addition, when ingredients are referred to as being "cold," "cool," "warm" or "hot," in nature, it is important to realize that this has nothing to do with temperature, but refers to certain concepts of traditional Chinese medicine. For example, medicine cold in nature is used for the treatment of heat symptom-complexes, such as impaired consciousness and maculation with high fever in acute infectious diseases. It is also used for bleeding due to existence of pathological heat, such as thrombocytopenic purpura, etc. Rhinocerus horn, antelope horn, and corn are ground into a fine powder, mixed with a decoction or administered for an emergency.

Medicine cool in nature is used for the treatment of symptoms of heat, marked by feverishness, flushed face, thirst, constipation, red tongue with rapid pulse, etc., such as *Rhizoma Coptidis* and *Flos Lonicerae*. These drugs have some antibacterial action and are used as antipyretic and antiinflammatory agents for pyogenic infections such as inflammations of the upper respiratory tract, boils, enteritis, dysentery, etc.

Medicine warm in nature is used to warm the meridians and dispel cold from within, such as *Fructus Piperis Longi* which is used to warm up the stomach. *Folium Artemisiae Argyi* and *Fructus Foeniculi* are used to warm up the uterus and testes, relieve pain in the lower abdomen, stop bleeding, etc.

Medicine hot in nature is used to treat cold symptom-complexes, such as lowered vital function, marked by general debility, low temperature, cold limbs, intolerance to cold, loose bowels, pallor, slow pulse, edema due to hypofunction of the kidneys, etc.

Radix Aconiti Praeparate, *Cortex Cinnamomi*, and *Rhizoma Zinggiberis* are drugs used as cardiotonics to restore the vital functioning of the heart and the kidneys in the treatment of collapse and shock.

1. TANGERINE JUJUBE DRINK

Function:

The large jujube or Chinese date contains protein, carbohydrates, organic acids, mucilage, vitamin A, B_2 and C, small quantities of calcium, phosphorus and iron. Laboratory tests have shown that the jujube can help strengthen the liver and muscles and help one gain weight. The large jujube is sweet in taste and mild in effect.

Tangerine peel contains volatile oils and flavones. Volatile oils can stimulate the digestive tract, thus causing gastric juices to flow and stimulating gastroenteric peristalsis. Tangerine peel is bitter in taste and mild in effect and may serve as a remedy for flatulence, cough, poor appetite and excess phlegm. The following recipe can particularly improve the appetite of older people. Frequent drinking after meals can help prevent or cure indigestion.

Preparation:

Fry 10 large red jujubes (Chinese dates) in a pan until they are burnt. Put them in a thermos glass together with 10 grams (over 3 ounces) of fresh tangerine peel or 3 grams (about ⅒ ounce) of dried tangerine peel. Infuse with boiling water for 10 minutes.

Note:

Frequent drinking before meals is good for increasing poor appetite, while frequent drinking after meals constitutes a remedy for indigestion.

2. SPECIAL CHRYSANTHEMUM TEA

Functions:

The chrysanthemum flower contains volatile oils, chrysanthamin, amino acid, ketones and small amounts of vitamin B_1. Chrysanthemum can strengthen the capillaries. 10 mg. of its extract is as effective as 2.5 mg. of rutin. A clinical test in China in which sixty-one patients of angina pectoris were observed, showed that Special Chrysanthemum Tea was very effective in 43.3% of the cases, and somewhat effective in 36.7% of the cases. Patients with less serious angina achieved even better results. The tea is also good, in various degrees, for shortness of breath, palpitation, panting, dizziness, headache and numbness of the limbs. In addition, steeped together with *flos sophorae*, it helps to cure hypertension. Among forty-six cases under observation, thirty-five cases showed alleviated symptoms of headache, dizziness and insomnia three to seven days after drinking the mix, followed by a return to normal blood pressure. The other eleven cases showed improvement in varied degrees ten to thirty days after drinking the mix. Chrysanthemum tastes bitter-sweet and according to Chinese medicine is "cool" in nature. It is a major tonic for refreshing the mind, sharpening the eyesight, promoting circulation and alleviating arthritis.

Flos sophorae is the flower of the Chinese Scholar or Locust tree. It contains rutin, sophorin A, B, and C. *Flos sophorae* can help strengthen the capillaries, reduce osmosis and increase elasticity of the blood vessels. Rutin helps dilate the coronary artery, improve blood circulation and can conspicuously bring down blood pressure. It also can reduce blood fat and prevent vascular sclerosis. Slightly bitter in taste and "cool" in nature, *flos sophorae* can reduce internal heat.

Preparation:

Place 3 grams (¹⁄₁₀ ounce) each of clean dried chrysanthemum, dried *flos sophorae* (flower of the Chinese Scholar Tree) and green tea in a porcelain mug and infuse with boiling water. Cover the mug tightly for 5 minutes.

Note:

Drink several times a day, to help relieve coronary disease and hypertension.

3. AUTUMN PEAR AND LOTUS ROOT JUICE

Function:

Autumn pear contains malic acid, citric acid, fructose, glucose, sucrose, etc. It is basically sweet with a slightly sour taste, and is "cool" in nature. It is a tasty fruit which can help produce saliva, moisten the respiratory tract and reduce internal heat and phlegm. Eating pears as often as possible can have a curative effect upon dry coughing.

Lotus root contains starch, protein, asparagin and vitamin C. It is sweet in taste and "cold" in nature. Eating it raw can reduce internal heat. Eating cooked lotus root can help invigorate the functioning of the spleen and increase the appetite. Lotus root is particularly good for dry cough in old people when it is prepared together with autumn pears, and is tasty as well.

Preparation:

Peel and core several autumn pears and remove the joints of an equal amount of lotus roots. Chop into small pieces. Then wrap the pears and roots in a piece of clean gauze and press or wring out the juice.

Note:

Drink the juice frequently without limit. It is good for chronic tracheitis in old people, coughing, purulent sputum, larynx xerosis, and xerostomia.

4. CONSOMME OF SILVER AND BLACK *TREMELLA*

Function:

Tremella is an edible fungus. Both silver and black *tremella* contain protein, fat, carbohydrates, ash content, phosphorus, iron, calcium, carotene, thiamine, riboflavin, nicotinic acid, mannan, mannose, glucose, xylose, glucuronic acid, and small amounts of pentose and methyl pentose. *Tremella* is sweet in taste and "mild" in nature. It can invigorate the body, improve functioning of the stomach, moisten the respiratory tract and keep the bowels free. Therefore it is suitable for patients of hypertension and constipation.

Preparation:

Soak and wash in warm water 10 grams (over ⅓ ounce) each of silver and black *tremella*. Place in a small bowl and add water and crystal sugar to taste. Steam for about an hour.

Note:

Remember to eat *tremella* as well as drink the soup. Take three times a day. The consomme is good for vascular sclerosis, hypertension and a type of eye hemorrhage.

5. MASHED WALNUT KERNEL SOAKED IN YELLOW WINE

Function:

The kernel of the walnut contains fat, protein, carbohydrates, nicotinic acid and vitamin B_1 and B_2. The walnut kernel is sweet in taste and "mild" in nature. It is a nourishing food which builds up vital energy, enriches the blood, moistens the respiratory tract and reduces phlegm. According to Chinese medicine classics, the walnut is an important remedy for invigorating the functioning of the liver and kidneys, and for toughening the muscles and bones. It can help alleviate lumbago, leg strains and pains in the muscles and bones, and can solidify the teeth and put a gloss in the hair.

Yellow wine is made from millet or rice (Shaoxing wine, which can be bought in any American Chinatown, will do), and is about 10% alcohol in content. It is usually used as an ingredient to enhance the efficacy of medicinal tonics.

Preparation:

Place 5 walnut kernels and 50 grams (nearly 2 ounces) of white sugar in an earthen bowl and mash with a rolling pin. Place in a pot, with 50 milliliters of yellow rice wine. Simmer over a low fire for 10 minutes. Take twice a day.

Note:

It is good for neurasthenia, insomnia, amnesia, and lumbago, leg aches and chronic constipation of older people.

6. GINSENG AND LOTUS SEED SOUP

Function:

Ginseng contains panaxoside, and is bitter-sweet in taste. Mild in nature, it is a rare medicinal herb and is used in Chinese medicine to build up vital energy, cure seminal emission, produce saliva, ease the mind, and soothe the nerves. According to clinical reports, ginseng has certain curative effects upon hypertension, myocardial dystrophy, coronary arteriosclerosis and angina pectoris. Ginseng is generally used as a tonic, as it can increase vital energy. Recent research has shown that ginseng can improve sexual functioning. Ginseng has more nutritive value when it is simmered together with lotus seeds and crystal sugar.

Preparation:

Place 10 grams of white ginseng and 10 lotus seeds (without hearts) in a small bowl and soak in water. Then add 30 grams (about 1 ounce) of crystal sugar and steam for an hour. Drink the soup and eat the lotus seeds. Keep the ginseng, adding more lotus seeds to it the next day and steam again. The ginseng can be used three times. The third time eat it together with the lotus seeds and broth.

Note:

This soup is good for hypertension, coronary heart disease, physical weakness, weak functioning of the spleen, emaciation, fatigue, spontaneous perspiration, loose bowels and impotence.

7. SNOW WHITE BROTH

Function:

Jellyfish contains protein, fat, carbohydrate, calcium, phosphorus, iron, thiamine, riboflavin and nicotinic acid. One kilo of dried jellyfish contains 1.32 grams of iodine. Laboratory tests on animals show that intravenous injections of 0.8–1.0 milliliter of decocted jellyfish extract into anaesthetized rabbits can bring down blood pressure. 82.6% of hypertension patients have shown improvement after using the broth as part of a program of clinical treatment, with better results attained with patients still at the earlier stages of the disease. Jellyfish is salty in taste and moderate in nature. It can help reduce phlegm as well as blood pressure.

Water chestnut contains starch, crude protein, fat, calcium, phosphorus, iron and vitamin C. Sweet in taste and "cold" in nature, it is good for excessive internal heat, diuresis and high blood pressure.

Preparation:

Soak and wash 30 grams (1 ounce) of dried jellyfish in lukewarm water. Then chop it into small pieces. Clean and peel 15 grams (½ ounce) of water chestnuts, and place in pot of water with jellyfish. Simmer over a low fire for an hour. Drink all of it at one time or divide it into several portions.

Note:

The broth is a remedy for hypertension, deficiency of *yin* (body fluids), coughing (due to chronic tracheitis caused by internal heat), xerostomia and larynx xerosis.

8. INSTANT DRINK OF *SHENQI* ESSENCE

Function:

Dangshen contains saponin, small amounts of alkaloids, sucrose, glucose, insulin and starch. Sweet in taste and moderate in nature, *Dangshen* can build up vital energy, produce saliva, and toughen muscles and bones.

Huang Qi, root of the milk vetch, contains sucrose, glucuronic acid, mucoitin and various amino acids. Sweet in taste and gentle in nature, *Huang Qi* is an important medicine for building up vital energy. Better results may be achieved in enriching vital energy if *Dangshen* is taken together with *Huang Qi*. Laboratory tests on animals show that both *Dangshen* and *Huang Qi* can bring down blood pressure.

Preparation:

Wash 250 grams (nearly 9 ounces) each of *Dangshen* (root of the *codonopsis pilosula*) and *Huang Qi* (*Astragalus reflexistipulus*). Soak in cold water until thoroughly expanded. Then boil for one and one-half hours, draining and reserving the decoction every thirty minutes. Then cook the decoction over a low fire until it is a sticky paste. Remove from fire and let stand. When it becomes lukewarm, add 500 grams (over 2 pounds) of white sugar so that any remaining liquid is absorbed. Mix well and dry. Then grind or crush into small pieces and store in a bottle for future use. Drink it in doses of 10 grams (over ⅓ ounce) dissolved in boiling water twice a day.

Note:

The drink is a remedy for palpitation and shortness of breath caused by deficient vital energy and poor appetite, unformed stool, prolapse of internal organs, edema, asthma and dizziness.

9. INSTANT DRINK FOR ALLEVIATING DIABETES

Function:

Winter melon contains protein, carbohydrates, crude fibre and vitamin C. Winter melon is light and sweet in taste and cool in nature. The winter melon is good chiefly as a diuretic.

Watermelon contains phosphoric acid, malic acid, fructose, glucose and vitamin C. Sweet in taste and cool in nature, watermelon is good for driving away summer heat, quenching one's thirst, and diuresis.

Preparation:

Take 1000 grams (over 2 pounds) each of fresh winter melon and watermelon skins and peel the hard outer skin and cut into thin slices. Crush 500 grams (over 1 pound) of the root of the Chinese *trichosanthes* and soak thoroughly in cold water. Place all the ingredients in a pot and decoct for an hour. Discard the residue and simmer the liquid over a low fire until condensed. Remove from fire when sticky and let stand. Add 500 grams (over 2 pounds) of white suger to absorb the remaining liquid when it becomes lukewarm. Mix well. Dry and crush to powder and store in a bottle. Drink it in doses of 10 grams (over ⅓ ounce) dissolved in boiling water several time a day.

Note:

The decoction is good for diabetes.

10. INSTANT *YUZHU* DRINK

Function:

Yuzhu contains cardinolides such as convalloside. It is sweet in taste and moderate in nature. Its main actions are to quench thirst and ease the heart and lung. In Chinese medicine, it is often used in preventing and treating coronary heart diseases and heart failure.

Preparation:

Wash 250 grams (nearly 9 ounces) of *Yuzhu* (Jade Bamboo in Chinese) and soak thoroughly in cold water. Then add an adequate amount of water* and decoct. Drain the decoction after twenty minutes and reserve. Add water and boil again. Repeat the boiling process three times. Then combine the three decoctions and continue to cook over a low flame until it becomes thick and sticky and nearly all the water in the decoction has evaporated. Let stand until lukewarm, then add 300 grams (10½ ounces) of white sugar to absorb all the remaining water. Mix thoroughly and dry, grinding to powder. Put the powder in a container for future use. Take it in doses of 10 grams (over ⅓ ounce) dissolved in boiling water three times daily.

Note:

Yuzhu is used in China for the treatment of rheumatic heart disease, pulmonary heart disease, coronary heart disease and heart failure.

11. INSTANT *LUOHANQUO* DRINK

Function:

Luohanquo (arhat fruit in Chinese) contains plentiful glucose and a substance 300 times as sweet as cane sugar which belongs to the triterpenoid family and is temporarily called "S-5." The "S-5" content of 15 grams of Luohanquo fruit is about 5%, and its sweetness equals that of 500 grams of cane sugar. *Luohanquo* is sweet in taste and cool in nature. It can counter excessive heat, refresh the lungs, relieve coughing

---

*The amount of water to be added to this and other recipes in this section depends greatly on personal taste. To obtain a stronger flavor, add less; to obtain a milder flavor, add more. How much is "adequate" is based on common sense or experience gained through practice.

and nourish the blood. *Luohanquo* is mainly used in treating diseases such as chronic pharyngitis, but people suffering from diabetes could benefit from it also. It is reported that *Luohanquo* can also reduce blood pressure. It is often used as a substitute for coffee.

Preparation:

Wash 250 grams (nearly 9 ounces) of *Luohanquo,* and crush into small pieces. Add water and boil. Drain the decoction after twenty minutes and reserve. Repeat the boiling process three times. Filter out the residue, combine the three decoctions and continue to boil over a low flame until it becomes thick and sticky and nearly all the water has evaporated. Let stand until it is lukewarm, and add 500 grams (over 1 pound) of white sugar to absorb the remaining water. Blend the sugar and the concentrate thoroughly, and dry. Then grind into powder and bottle for future use. Take in doses of 10 grams (over ⅓ ounce) dissolved in boiling water. Drink as often as you like.

Note:

It can be used in the treatment of acute and chronic pharyngitis, laryngitis and hypertension.

12. SESAME WALNUT TOFFEE

Function:

Brown cane sugar is the brown crystal refined from the juice of the stem of the sugar cane plant. Its functions are similar to those of white cane sugar. Black sesame and walnut kernel are tonics and can help to lubricate the intestines, improve the blood circulation, strengthen the liver and kidneys and stop premature greying of the hair. Frequent eating of Sesame Walnut Toffee can prevent chronic constipation and vascular sclerosis among old people.

Preparation:

Put 500 grams (over 1 pound) of brown cane sugar in a pot, add a little water and cook over a low flame until thick and sticky. Then add 250 grams (nearly 9 ounces) each of roasted black sesame and roasted walnut kernel and stir thoroughly. Pour immediately (while still hot) into a large enamel plate which has been greased. When the mixture cools down a little, press into a flat cake and cut into small pieces. Stand and let cool completely.

Note:

The toffee serves as a tonic for the brain and kidneys and is good for the hair. Frequent and large doses can treat neurasthenia, amnesia, prematurely greying hair and baldness.

13. HONEY HAW

Function:

Haw is the fruit of the Hawthorn tree. It contains tartaric acid, citric acid, crategolac acid, tannic acid, malic acid, saponin, fructose, vitamin C, protein and lipide. It is both sweet and sour in taste and a little warm in nature. When in the stomach, it can increase the actions of enzymes and help digest meats. Drinking haw juice after meals can aid digestion. As it can lower blood pressure, stimulate the heart, dilate the blood vessels and reduce the cholesterol content of the blood, it is a favorite fruit of the aged in China.

Preparation:

Wash 500 grams (over 1 pound) of raw haw, tear off the stalks, and core. Then place in an aluminum pot, add water and boil until 70% cooked. When there is nearly no water in the pot, add 250 grams (nearly 9 ounces) of honey and continue to boil over a low flame until well done. Stop cooking when the liquid is fully absorbed. Stand and let cool, then place in a container for future use.

Note:

Honey Haw increases the appetite, clears up indigestion caused by eating too much meat, stops loose bowels, invigorates blood circulation and removes blood stasis. Taking it before meals can improve the appetite. Taking it after meals can cure indigestion caused by eating too much meat. Eating honey haw in large quantities can aid in the treatment of diarrhea, coronary heart disease and discomfort around the heart and chest.

14. SOUP OF CHINESE YAM, MILK AND MUTTON

Function:

Mutton contains protein, lipide, carbohydrates, inorganic salt and various vitamins. Mutton is warm in nature and is a tonic for warming up the internal organs, improving weak health, increasing the appetite and building up strength.

Chinese Yam contains saponin, mucilage, choline, starch, glycoprotein and free amino acids. Sweet in taste and moderate in nature, Chinese Yam is nourishing and good for the health. This soup is particularly useful in nursing older people in poor health.

Preparation:

Wash one piece of mutton weighing 500 grams (over 1 pound) and place in pot. Add 25 grams (under 1 ounce) of fresh ginger and cook over a low flame for half a day. Remove one bowl of the broth, add 100 grams (3.5 ounces) of peeled, cleaned and sliced Chinese Yam and place both in another pot. Cook until well done, then add half a bowl of milk and a little bit of table salt. Heat to a boil and remove from flame.

Note:

Frequent eating of this soup can strengthen a weak constitution. It can be used to treat poor circulation to the limbs, cold sweat, exhaustion, shortness of breath, dryness in the mouth, restlessness and insomnia after illness and child delivery.

15. *FULING* CAKE

Function:

Fuling is the dried nucleus of *porio cocos* which is a porous fungus. It contains B-Poria-polysacchrose and such triterpenoids as pachynic acid and tumulosic acid. *Fuling* is sweet and light in taste and moderate in nature. It can filtrate unnecessary liquids in the body and functions as a diuretic. It can also improve the functioning of the spleen, regulate the stomach and tranquilize the nerves. Eating a little *Fuling* cake frequently can help treat nocturnal emission and amnesia as well as vital energy deficiency, weakness, palpitation and shortness of breath.

Preparation:

Mix equal amounts of pulverized *Fuling*, rice flour and white sugar. Add water and mix into batter. Then make very thin pancakes with the batter in a flat-bottom pan with low heat.

Note:

Fuling cake benefits the stomach and improves the vital energy. Frequent eating of this cake helps treat such ailments as vital energy deficiency, weakness, palpitation, shortness of breath, poor appetite, neurasthenia, insomnia, dropsy and watery stool.

16. TURNIP DUMPLINGS

Function:

Turnip contains glucose, saccharose, fructose, methylsulfhyrate and vitamin C. Turnip is hot in taste and cool in nature and is both a common vegetable and an effective herbal medicine. In China it is referred to as "the king of medicines in easing the flow of vital energy." Its main actions are to clear up indigestion, reduce pyretic phlegm, ease the flow of vital energy and comfort the internal organs. It is reported that drinking turnip juice can prevent gall-stones from forming. Turnip dumpling is a delicious and appetizing food as well.

Preparation:

Wash and shred several white turnips. Then stir-fry in vegetable oil until half done. Add some minced grilled pork and blend to use as dumpling filling. Make dough for the dumplings with flour and water. Roll out and divide the dough into small circles. Place filling on each circle, roll up and bake in a pan until done.*

Note:

Turnip pancake benefits the stomach, eases the flow of vital energy, aids digestion, reduces phlegm and is good for those suffering from poor appetite, indigestion, bloatedness after eating, chronic coughing and asthma.

17. SOUP OF EEL, *DANGGUI* AND *DANGSHEN*

Function:

Eel contains protein, lipide, inorganic salts and vitamins. It is moderate in nature and is a good tonic to build up vital energy and blood. It also helps relieve weakness and make up for losses of body fluids.

Danggui and *Dangshen* are plant roots often used in Chinese medicine. *Danggui* is sweet and hot in taste and moderate in nature. It is an important medicine in building up and harmonizing the blood. *Dangshen* is sweet in taste and mod-

---

*Electric and gas ranges are not widely used in China. When baking is done, someone will always be there to keep watch.

erate in nature and is an important medicine in improving vital energy. The decoction of eel, *Danggui* and *Dangshen* can invigorate the body's vital energy and blood and is particularly helpful in preparing tonics for older people.

Preparation:

Wash and clean 500 grams (over 1 pound) of eel, discarding head, bones and internal organs. Cut into long, thin strips. Then add 15 grams (½ ounce) each of *Danggui* and *Dangshen*, wrapped in a piece of gauze and a fair amount of water. Cook for an hour and take out the gauze bag. Then add salt, scallion and ginger to taste. Consume the soup and the eels over several meals.

Note:

This soup can build up vital energy or blood, increase strength, help relieve weakness after long illness, alleviate exhaustion, feebleness and emaciation.

18. *LONGAN* LIQUOR

Function:

Longan pulp contains vitamin B, glucose, saccharose, tartaric acid, protein and lipide. *Longan* pulp is sweet in taste and moderate in nature. It functions to whet the appetite and is a tonic for the spleen, heart and brain. It can also help greatly in soothing the nerves and enriching the blood. Old people suffering from general weakness find it especially refreshing prepared with eggs.

Preparation:

Place 200 grams (7 ounces) of clean *longan* pulp in a narrow-necked bottle. Add about 400cc of 60 proof spirits and seal the bottle. Shake once daily. It will be ready to use in half a month. Drink ten to twenty cc each time, twice daily.

Note:

Longan liquor warms and nourishes the heart and spleen and has a refreshing effect. It is also applicable to treatment of debility, insomnia, amnesia and palpitation.

19. SWEETENED FRESH *LONGAN*

Function:

See recipe #18

Preparation:

Shell and core 500 grams (over 1 pound) of fresh *longan* and place in a porcelain bowl. Then add 50 grams (nearly 2 ounces) of white sugar, steam and let cool. Repeat the steaming and cooling process several times until the *longans* turn black. Finally, add a little more white sugar, blend and put in a container for future use.

Note:

Sweetened Fresh *Longan* is said to be more effective than Ginseng and other potent herbs as it helps build up vital energy and blood. Frequent eating of Sweetened Fresh *Longan* can help alleviate weakness, emaciation, insomnia, palpitation and amnesia, act as a tonic for the aged, strengthen women before delivery and help restore health after illness.

20. PRAWN LIQUOR

Function:

Although prawns can be found in rivers and lakes, those referred to here are sea prawns. The main action of Prawn Liquor is to build up the kidneys and increase vital energy.

Preparation:

Wash a pair of big, fresh prawns and place in a wide-mouth bottle or porcelain jar. Then add 250 cc of 60 proof spirits and seal the container. Soak the prawns in the liquor for one week. Drink the liquor daily according to one's capacity.

Note

Prawn Liquor can also go with meals. When the liquor is finished, cook the prawns and eat them over several meals. Prawn liquor can be used for the treatment of sexual dysfunction and impotence.

21. STEAMED SILVER CARP STUFFED WITH TEA LEAVES

Function:

Silver carp meat contains protein, fat, carbohydrates, inorganic salt and vitamins. It has mild medicinal properties and can invigorate the central organs and help relieve flatulence. It is used mainly for the treatment of general debility. When steamed, its meat is especially delicious and can stimulate one's appetite. And when taken with little or no salt, it is also effective in the treatment of chronic nephritis and edema.

Preparation:

Remove the viscera and gills of a one-pound silver carp but leave the scales. Stuff it full with tea leaves (green tea), and steam till well done. Add only a little salt.

Note:

Silver carp is a nourishing food that can build up health and quench thirst. It is also good for the treatment of fever, diabetes or any ailment for which frequent drinking and urination are symptoms.

22. CARP COOKED WITH GARLIC AND GINGER

Function:

Carp meat contains protein, fat, calcium, phosphorus, iron and vitamins. Carp is one of the most delicious fishes and is considered a delicacy in China. It has the same nutritional effect as the silver carp. Cooked with garlic and vinegar, it is appealing not only in taste, but also in color as well as in fragrance.

Preparation:

Take a carp of fair size, remove the scales, gills and intestines, wash clean and cut it into pieces. Fry in vegetable oil till brown. Then add water, soy sauce, sugar and yellow rice wine to taste, and stew till well done with just a little sauce left. Place the fish onto a plate, and sprinkle on it diced ginger, garlic and a little vinegar before being served.

Note:

This dish is nutritious and helps relieve flatulence. It is therefore good for patients suffering from poor health, persistent coughing, asthma, indigestion and heart-burn.

23. STEWED CHICKEN WITH MALTOSE

Function:

Chicken meat contains protein, fat, calcium, phosphorus, iron, vitamin B_1, vitamin B_2 and nicotinic acid. It has mild medicinal properties and can invigorate the central organs, restore vital energy and replenish bone marrow. Therefore, it is commonly given to patients during convalescence. Stewed hen with maltose is even more nutritious.

Preparation:

Wash one hen, removing the viscera. Stuff with 30 grams (1 ounce) of dried rhizome of rehmannia (*Rehmannia glutinosa*), scallion, ginger and a little salt, then pour in 100 grams (3.5 ounces) of maltose and stitch up the opening. Place the hen in an aluminum pot with the opening facing up, then add water and stew over low heat till well-done.

Note:

Stewed maltose chicken is an effective nourishing food and is especially good for people suffering from emaciation, low fever, night sweat, and poor health due to long illness.

24. STEWED DUCK WITH *CORDYCEPS SINENSIS*

Function:

Duck meat contains protein, fat, carbohydrates, calcium, phosphorus, iron and vitamins, and has nutritional effects similar to that of chicken meat.

Cordyceps sinensis is also known as Chinese caterpillar fungus, and contains fat, crude protein, coarse fibre and carbohydrates. Stewed duck with *Cordyceps sinensis* is a time-honored tonic in the provinces of southern China.

Preparation:

Wash one duck, removing the viscera. Place in an earthenware or aluminum pot. Add 5 to 10 pieces of *Cordyceps sinensis* with a little salt, ginger, scallion and water. Then stew over a low heat till it is well cooked.

Note:

This stew can strengthen the constitution and increase vital energy. It is therefore considered an ideal tonic for people suffering from general debility after long illness, cold sweats, poor circulation to the limbs, impotence and seminal emission.

25. BABY DOVE STEAMED WITH *BEIQI* (*ASTRAGALUS MEMBRANACEUS*) AND *JIZI* (*LYCIUM SINENSIS*)

Function:

Astragalus membranaceus is the root of the membranous milk vetch which contains choline, betaine, amino acid, sucrose, glucronic acid and folic acid. It functions as a cardiac stimulant, diuretic and can lower blood pressure. It tastes sweet and is very mild in nature. It can also invigorate the spleen, help stop excessive sweating and build up vital energy.

Lycium sinensis is the fruit of the Chinese wolfberry which contains carotene, vitamin B_1, vitamin B_2, nicotinic acid and vitamin C. Its main functions are to reduce blood sugar content and blood pressure. *Lycium sinensis* is used often as a traditional tonic in Chinese medicine for its bitter-sweet taste and mild nature.

The meat of baby doves is rich, tender and nourishing. The above three ingredients, when cooked together, are good especially for people suffering from general debility after illness.

Preparation:

Remove the feathers and viscera from a newly-hatched baby dove or pigeon. Place in a bowl with 30 grams (1 ounce) each of *Beiqi* and *Jizi* and add an adequate amount of water. Steam till done. Remember to consume the broth as well as the meat.

Note:

Taken once every three days, it is effective in the treatment of general debility after long illness, lassitude, inertia and sweating.

26. PARTRIDGE COOKED WITH *YUZHU* (*POLYGONALUM OFFICINALE*)

Function:

Yuzhu comes from the root of a plant that is a member of the lily family. It contains convallamarin, nicotinic acid, chelidonic acid and vitamin A and is effective as a cardiac stimulant. Partridge meat is sweet in taste and mild in nature. It can serve to invigorate the central organs and build up the physique.

Preparation:

Remove the feathers and viscera from a partridge. Place in a pot and steam it with 15 grams (½ ounce) of *Yuzhu* till done.

Note:

Taken two to three times, it may be effective in the treatment of weakness and coughing due to pulmonary tuberculosis, afternoon flush, senile heart disease caused by coronary sclerosis, excessive phlegm due to rheumatic heart disease and other causes.

27. PIG'S FEET COOKED WITH OCTOPUS

Function:

Octopus meat functions to enrich the blood and invigorate the body's vital energy. Sweet and salty in taste, pig's feet is also mild in nature and can enrich the blood as well as stimulate lactation. Pig's feet cooked with octopus is a delicacy in China and is especially good for people of advanced age who suffer from poor health and weakness.

Preparation:

Cook 120 grams (4 ounces) of dried octopus and one or two pig's feet in water over a low flame until the broth becomes thick. Remember to drink the broth as well as eat the meat. Serve alone or together with other dishes.

28. BULL'S GENITALS COOKED WITH *JIZI (LYCIUM SINENSIS)*

Function:

Lycium sinensis is the fruit of the Chinese wolfberry and functions to invigorate the liver and kidneys, strengthen the bones and replenish marrow. The external genital organs of a bull include the penis and the two testicles. It functions to increase virility and strengthen the kidneys, and is especially good for men suffering from impotence.

Preparation:

Place the external genital organs of a bull and 20–40 grams (.7–1.4 ounces) of *Jizi* in a bowl and steam them till well-done. Consume the meat as well as the juice. While steaming, add two pieces of ginger to get rid of the rank smell.

Note:

This recipe may be used as a tonic for the aged and is generally prescribed for people who suffer from general weakness, kidney debility, pain in back and legs, seminal emission, impotence and excessive nocturnal urination.

29. PIG'S BRAIN COOKED WITH CHINESE YAM AND *JIZI*

Function:

Chinese yam is an important ingredient in traditional Chinese medicine for its tonic effects on the spleen, kidneys and the vital energy of the body. It tastes sweet and is mild in nature. If taken frequently, it helps invigorate the central organs, build up strength and promote muscle growth. It also is good for improving the functioning of the eyes and ears.

Jizi, which is sweet in taste and mild in nature, also builds up vital energy and helps improve the functioning of the spleen, kidneys and eyes. Because of its tonic effect on vital energy and virility, *Lycium sinensis* is liable to cause sexual excitement, hence the saying in China: "Do not take "Lycium Sinensis" when far far away from home." Pig's brain cooked together with Chinese yam and *Jizi* is a nutritious delicacy for the aged for its tonic effects on the kidneys and brain.

Preparation:

Stew one pig's brain, 30 grams (1 ounce) of Chinese yam and 10 grams (⅓ ounce) of *Jizi* in water over a low flame.

Note:

This recipe is used mainly to treat senile weakness, dizziness, headache and neurasthenia.

30. GLUTINOUS RICE COOKED IN COCONUT

Function:

Coconut meat tastes sweet and is mild in nature, and contains fat, protein, carbohydrates and many vitamins. It can cure general debility, invigorate vital energy and build up health. Glutinous rice helps to invigorate the central organs and revitalize the body. Steamed together, glutinous rice and coconut can rejuvenate the functioning of the brain.

Preparation:

Wash some glutinous rice, and pour into a coconut which has been cut open on top (do not remove the coconut milk). Then put the top of the coconut on again and steam for about three hours. Eat both the rice and the coconut meat.

Note:

This recipe is known for its tonic effects on the brain and complexion.

Glossary

baihui point	intersection of the line formed between the tips of the ears and the central line of the head (See Fig. 262)
bow step	movement in exercise where you bend your right or left knee and straighten the opposite leg
cudgel	a straight piece of hard wood, 8 inches long and 1 inch in diameter with convex ends; used to perform certain sets of exercises
Dailing points	inside of wrists
dantian	point located one inch to 1½ inches below the navel; see also *qihai*
empty step	raise heel of left or right foot off the floor leaving the rest of foot down
guanyuan point	point 3 inches below the navel
hegu	the part of the hand between the thumb and index finger; also called *hukou*
hypertension	high blood pressure
hypotension	low blood pressure
inner *loagong*	the palm of the hand
laogong	the inner and outer points of the hand
meridians	passages through which vital energy circulates and along which the acupuncture points are distributed

middle *dantian*	same as *dantian:* point 1½ inches below the navel
obliquely	at a slant
occipital bone	a compound bone of the skull at the back of each ear
outer *laogong*	point at back of the hand
qihai point	middle *dantian:* 1½ inches below the navel
ren mai	central line of the abdomen and chest
scores of times	approximately 40 to 50 times—always remembering to forget exact counts
seven human emotions	anger, joy, brooding, melancholy, sorrow, fear, shock; emotions which should be avoided
shanzhong point	point in front of the chest
shenyu point	point on the back 1½ inches from the 14th vertebrae
tenosynovitis	inflammation of a tendon sheath
upper *dantian*	point between the eyebrows; *yintang*
Xinhuo	a type of internal heat
Xuhuo	a type of internal heat
Yamen point	point at the back of the neck
Yang	masculine or positive principle in nature; in reference to the body—vital energy
Yin	female or negative principle in nature; in reference to the body—body fluids
yintang point	point between the eyebrows; upper *dantian*
yongquan points	points at arch of the feet